MONASTERY WITHOUT WALLS

Daily Life in the Silence

Monastery Without Walls

Daily Life in the Silence

Bruce Davis, Ph.D.

CELESTIAL ARTS
BERKELEY, CALIFORNIA

I wish to thank my wife and partner, family, friends, many retreat participants and teachers for the love and inspiration for this book. I want to particularly thank my friends at Celestial Arts for the support which made this book possible.

Copyright © 1990 by Bruce Davis, Ph.D. All rights reserved. No part of this book may be reproduced in any form, except for brief review, without the written permission of the publisher.

CELESTIAL ARTS
P.O. Box 7327
Berkeley, California 94707

Cover design by Ken Scott
Cover photo by Noeleke Glenn Klavers
Cover inset photo: lotus flower by Gunter Vierow
Text design and composition by Jeff Brandenburg, ImageComp

Library of Congress Cataloging-in-Publication Data

Davis, Bruce, 1950–
    Monastery without walls : daily life in the silence / Bruce Davis.
        p.   cm.
    ISBN 0-89087-593-6 : $7.95
        1. Silence—Religious aspects—Christianity. 2. Solitude—
    Religious aspects—Christianity. 3. Spiritual life. I. Title.
    BV4509.5.D25   1990
    248.8'8—dc20   89-28698
                                                                    CIP

First Printing, 1990

Manufactured in the United States of America

0   9   8   7   6   5   4   3   2

96   95   94   93   92   91   90

CONTENTS

INTRODUCTION

Life's peak moments: alone in nature, in the arms of a lover, immersed in a project, on vacation or spiritual retreat could all be seen as moments of intimate silence. Each day is more complete when the moment of silence comes. Suddenly all our senses are pulled to the present, to the silent perfection within us and around us. This perfection, this instant of beauty, occupies more than our minds and touches more than our feelings. In some inexplicable way we are reminded that we have a soul and we are loved. Such moments are how we imagine monks and mystics feel much of the time cloistered in monasteries.

Like monks and mystics, we thirst for this creative silence. Yet we also choose to have families and jobs, a life very much in the world. The monk or mystic inside us knows there is holiness in solitude that gives meaning to all activity. Without the opportunity for quiet reflection inside, the busy life outside is empty and fruitless.

Somehow the extraordinary moments when time seemingly stops and life's unique presence is felt must become more available to us. These moments of sacred silence can become an everyday experience if we learn to be with them, ii

if we learn to live in the monastery, the monastery without walls.

————

The monastery without walls recognizes the human need for silence, the part of life that includes the peacefulness of solitude, where the roots of what is sacred can take hold in the soul. The monastery without walls represents the human desire to find one's own spiritual path, one's own divinity as well as the divinity in others; to practice the rich path of meditation and prayer; to live the life of simplicity and humility from which true wholeness can emerge. Today's monastery extends beyond the traditional walls, because so many people feel a hunger for spiritual purpose yet know we cannot separate ourselves from the cares and joys of the world. Many voices in nature, in the world, in ourselves, are crying out, calling for our attention. But in each cry and call, perhaps there is a common plea for us to come back to the sense of the sacred, to come home once again to the silence.

CHAPTER ONE

SILENCE

THE CRY FOR SILENCE

The twentieth century may go down in history as the one in which we lost the silence. Since the industrial revolution, the noise of machines has increasingly filled our homes, cities, farms, skies, and earth. Even the silence of the most remote forests has been penetrated by the daily sonic booms of high-flying machines. A place of true silence is becoming more and more rare.

The noise of technology filling our lives goes mostly unnoticed, as if it were normal. But it was not too many years ago that the loudest sound typically came from children at play, a waterfall or a neighbor's dog barking at a rabbit. Nature and living creatures filled the air with their desires and needs, or the air was still. Human sounds or the sounds of nature; the wind, thunder, and ocean would be heard. Nature's many voices would rise and fall out of the silence. Each sound would have a cause and effect that could easily be understood. Nature's sounds represented the changing seasons, terrain, and abundant life in the silence. What filled the air would give witness to the presence of

1

silence in all living things. It was not too long ago that all sound would emerge and then disappear. Life was grounded in silence. There was little or no noise that interfered. There was silence and there were nature's sounds coming out of the silence.

The loss of daily silence would not be so profound if we did not need its life-giving qualities so much. It is common these days to hear someone say, "I cannot hear myself think." If life has become so noisy that we cannot hear ourselves think, how can we hear the calling of our soul? Is it any wonder that so many people think and live as if they don't have a soul?

Noise has taken over our homes, neighborhoods, and places of rest, recreation, and healing. Noise has taken over where there was once only pure sounds of nature and the presence of life. Instead of listening to the voices of our inner selves, other people, and nature, we spend much more time listening to the noise of radios, televisions, and other machines. Although modern technology has made our lives more convenient, it has threatened our ability to listen inside, to hear each other. It is easier for us to turn on the remote control and be passively entertained. The richness of our inner lives will be lost and forgotten if machines continue to seduce us with their promises to improve our lives. As they drive us to buy more, consume more, and look better, they intrude on and limit our being, preventing us from finding meaning in who we are and what we do.

The absence of daily peace and quiet critically challenges the state of the human psyche, family, community, and the planet. One of the most common complaints therapists hear from their patients is that they feel depressed, separate from themselves and those about them. When will we recognize that the noise we live with has dulled and fragmented our world, detached us from ourselves?

The love available in the silence is unknown. The intimate stillness has been lost. The simple silence that restores our center, our core of being, is endangered. What refuges of peace and quiet we do find we do not know how to enjoy.

Real peace disturbs most of us. We do not know what to do with it. We want to be busy. We feel uncomfortable when there isn't some noise filling the air. We desire peace so much yet we are afraid of it. Perhaps we are fearful because silence has become so foreign, unknown. Noise and stress have become such fixtures in our world that if we are not personally overwhelmed by them, we constantly hear through the media of those who are. We have lived with the threat of so much violence that the tenderness of silence has become less and less believable and more and more difficult to find and experience.

There is a positive side to losing the silent world within and around us and that is the value we are beginning to place upon it. Many people have begun to hold the silence as precious, even holy, although they hardly know it. A century ago there was so much opportunity for experiencing silence that few people were aware of how important it was. Silence was everywhere. Then, in relatively very few years, it disappeared and hardly anyone cried out. Except for such critics as Henry David Thoreau and John Muir, the noise went unchallenged. Those who did cry out were considered old fashioned, remote, and against progress. In truth they had found their home in the silence and had to suffer its gradual disappearance.

Then, as now, few people knew how to express their appreciation of the silent beauty in all life. Until this century, human history benefited from the presence of silence to naturally restore the human psyche. Silence just was, and humankind could feel interrelated with all of nature. Our interdependence with every living thing was constantly reinforced by the silence. This reinforcement is what is quickly leaving our consciousness. The current crises on the planet can serve to make us appreciate many things we previously took for granted, including many species that are now endangered and the weather, which appears to be changing. However, neither endangered species nor changing weather patterns may be more important than the loss of the silence.

In the past, silence reigned and all creatures conformed to the rules of nature. In most cultures, people who wanted to live closer to the silence either moved together into communities like monasteries or simply wandered off into nature. Many people quite naturally opened to the silent wonder inside themselves and lived simply in the quiet world. They did not need monasteries, nature preserves, and other temples of silence as much, because the opportunity for solitude and solace was nearly everywhere. Now that silence is scarce not only are all remaining places of silence sacred, but also sacred are an understanding of the mysteries of the silence and the possible insights gained from living with the silence. Such understanding and insight should be saved from being completely forgotten.

The cry for silence first began when we sought the intimacy of our mother's breast. It came in the times we longed for family outings in nature or wanted to lie with our parents in bed at night. The silence is remembered as something we wanted to share but never quite could. There seemed to be no one who cared to help us understand how the silence felt. Or it simply was something that was not discussed. Yet the silence was real. The cry would come again and again, and we would hope for someone to come and listen with us, someone to share all the wonderful feelings the silence seemed to hold secret within itself.

The cry for the silence is in us. It is the cry of our original voice, the divine joy before the womb. It is the cry of each soul that carries the memory of love's perfect body, silence. It is the cry from the place in each of us where creation begins. We sense that we cannot afford to lose the silence because we would lose contact with our innermost self, our contact with eternity.

The cry for silence is for every cry that goes unheard.
The silence is the last great ocean, receiving all wishes
large and small. If the silence ends, it means no one is
listening and only night is left to fall.

THE SEARCH FOR SILENCE

Today people everywhere are searching for the peace and the love that are found in the silence. We save our money and vacation time, travel long distances, go to great lengths to find the peace and quiet. And when we do, we are overly anxious to feel and enjoy it. We want to catch each moment of stillness and hold onto it, knowing it may be some time before we have peace and quiet again. We long for the silence and are afraid to lose it once we find it.

People try many routes to silence. Traditionally it was believed that when someone developed a special thirst for the silence, it was necessary to leave "the world" and go inside the stone walls of a monastery. There the perfect soundlessness would lead the person to the Intimate Being. But monks and nuns through the ages have learned that it is not so easy to detach themselves from worldly desires, worldly noise, no matter how physically separate they were from them. Worldly customs and habits are difficult to give up. Monks and nuns found that their inner world was still attracted to the outside world, which was what they wanted to leave behind.

Physical separation is no guarantee in our search for silence and is only one possible tool. Whether we are in a monastery, alone in nature, or in a busy crowd, the silence has to be opened to and appreciated. And it is in our possible relationship to the silent world that we discover the sacred.

The search for silence can occur during the course of each day and includes many silent encounters and quiet meetings. If we are willing, our daily routine, our work, relationships, and moments eating, exercising, and being alone can each be part of the perfect route, one moment at a time, one encounter with silence after another. Life's many different faces all contain the silence. As we open and reveal ourselves in the stillness, the many faces of the silence are unveiled to us. Between our inner and outer worlds is the silence. The silence is the great intermediary. Within, around, and through our inner life and the outside world is the sea of the immaterial, the uncharted silent vastness.

The silence is the home of God. As we search within ourselves to find our place in the great stillness, we discover the room that has been held for each of us, our place in the vast world of silence. As we commit ourselves to receive the simple presence in our lives, we are opening to feel God's presence, which is the presence of love.

The search for the silence is often limited by the names we give to it. But silence is greater than any name, term, or pronoun we may use to describe it and any image we may attach to it. He is beyond measure. She is more than love as we know love. The silence called by many names is limited in every attempt to address it. Although scores of monks and mystics have traveled to the silent kingdom and settled in it, only our own experience will yield just the right map for each of us to follow. Only our own efforts will uncover the golden meaning in the words that we use for describing and searching for silence.

Organized in various religions, in different groups on many paths, we are often more attached to "our beliefs," "our way," than to risk more, surrendering more, loving more, letting go of our images, so that the silence, God, can be fresh and alive within us. The silence is more than our ideas, more than our recent experiences. The silence is ever newly with us!

In our search for silence, attaching any name to the great quiet may simply be an act of arrogance, trying to find some limited safety in front of the immense mystery. The silence gives us all shelter. Some of us think of this shelter in terms of family and friends or the town or city where we live. Some of us find shelter in the vastness through the church, where we get to know the silence in an orderly, accepted tradition. But whatever life we create for ourselves, whether in business, teaching, parenting, or simply seeking, it is all in the lucid stillness. The identity we create for ourselves and give meaning to every day is made inside the silence and is possible only because of the infinite, silent cooperation and support. The voiceless world is so empty, so giving, that it can be all things to all people, invisible yet visibly full of life's many blessings.

In their search for silence many people often seem reluctant to enter into the unknown. They think that the silence is simply vacant, nothing, the absence of noise and substance. But even though the quiet presence cannot be taken apart and put under a microscope or viewed from a telescope, even though we cannot reduce it to atomic particles or expand it into planets and galaxies, it is no less present. Just as everyone who is in love knows love's reality, including love's wonder and joy, love's tests and disappointments, the silence blooms into life as we develop a relationship with it. As the lover must risk his or her heart to know love's riches, we must risk our hearts to the silence in order to know its beauty. For centuries intellectuals have approached the great love, God's presence in the silence, and scholars have argued about it. But the people who have sought the silence with their hearts and souls, their bodies as well as their minds, have opened themselves to the place of exquisite harmony. They have come to know the silent divinity by allowing the silence to touch them.

The search for silence grows easier as we develop a relationship with it. The more distant a relationship we have with the silence, the more likely we are to fear it. The less developed our relationship, the more overwhelming are our feelings of nothingness. Meanwhile, the perfect stillness receives all that we do and feel, everything we think and care about. The silence takes everything we offer, from our smallest thoughts to our greatest plans, and makes room for all of it. The silence gives us empty space to create and invites us to feel the support that is present for us.

In our search for silence we find a path in the stillness through the people we live with, the rooms we live in. Every relationship has a unique presence of silence. The child, the mother, the friend, and the neighbor all carry a special quality of silence. The earth in all its varied terrain is filled with the presence of silence. Each mountain is a mountain of silence. Each river carries the silence downstream. The deserts and great plains stretch to the horizons of the silence. The earth looks out to the sky where clouds, moon, sun, planets, and stars give body to silence. And underneath the sky every creature, every plant, and every flower is a blossom of silence. Every day the world emerges out of the quiet. All of life is born out of the quiescence, full of invitations to return to the source where we find ourselves surrounded in perfect, sacred silence.

In our search for silence we discover that many of the remaining refuges of peace and quiet are under attack. Whether we are speaking of nature reserves or the world's remaining monasteries, they are being questioned: Is this monastery necessary to modern life or is it a relic from a bygone era? Is this forest reserved for nature an obstruction to development? Monasteries are disappearing as fewer and fewer people preserve the spiritual tradition that holds the silence sacred. Refuges of stillness are being judged quickly and harshly, and thought to be out of touch with modern needs. But it is exactly the opposite: The time has come for us to recognize that the last refuges of silence are exactly what the world needs. As nature wrestles for survival, monasteries and the monk and mystic inside us are wrestling for survival, for an authentic spiritual identity.

THE MONASTERY

Monasteries and spiritual communities of all religions share a history of collecting silence for the benefit of the world's soul. Their monks and nuns have risked a life of contemplation in a world that demands action. Small islands in the midst of the world's busyness, monasteries have been safe places to chart the course of the interior life, the life full of silence. And throughout history, every spiritual seeker has faced the temptation of being seduced into action, into any form of pleasure or restlessness that takes him or her away from the silent path of prayer and devotion. Monasteries of all religions are the historic places where the quietudes have been searched for and lived with.

Today in the search for silence, we run into many of society's questions that stand at the monastery's front door, threatening the survival of these historic schools for silence. As society is questioning, the sensitive people in monasteries are also questioning: What is the individual's responsibility for the world's problems? How is sexuality to be integrated into daily life and our life's purpose? What are friendship and true intimacy? How do the needs for personal freedom find their place with respect to the needs of the community? These among many other questions are knocking hard on the doors of monasteries everywhere. But in truth, these questions are knocking on everyone's door. The monk and mystic inside us who is close to the silence hears the knocks more loudly. But before surrendering to the noise at the front door, we should remember the tradition that has survived the ages. Let's go to the well of silence and allow the depths of truth to answer the questions for us.

The search for silence lies in the depths of our being. In the heart of every monk and mystic is the biblical saying, "Go and sell all you have, give to the poor, and come." This saying scares away many people because it makes them feel intimidated, incapable of joining the company of the saints. The invitation of the silence in this calling has been lost and fears have remained instead. When we are invited to "go and sell all we have," we are called to give up our attachments to things we hold onto as important and to depend upon the silence for what is truly important in life. And when we are invited to "give to the poor and come," we are called to give to the poor before us, giving to our own experience of spiritual poverty and that in others. In other words, we are called to love where love is most needed.

The invitation to 'go and sell all you have and come' is an invitation to let go of our complex identity and come to a new commitment to what is central in life, to what gives life meaning. The invitation for the monastic in everyone is to center life around the silence, the invisible, the unknown, so their truth can be found.

The search for silence has been in the hearts of aware beings throughout history. The purpose of silence opens as we open to make a complete commitment so that the quiet presence can be our all and everything. Making this commitment is central for every monk or mystic. It turns the part of each of us that is seeking into fully being, giving life to the soul by making the soul the purpose for living.

The search for silence through prayer, work, and community for spiritual teachers, wise men, holy women, saints known and unknown, is not so different from the search for true prayer, work, and community that we all face. Inside monasteries around the world, monks and mystics are facing the challenges that the monk or mystic inside us also faces sooner or later in our own monasteries without walls.

Prayer

The thirst for silence has always been satisfied by prayer. But true prayer is not so easy to find. We think that if only we could give up everything, and live like a monk or a nun we could have the inner stillness necessary for prayer. But we don't want to give up everything so we settle for less than a life full of the purity of silence. In fact monks and nuns do not easily find pure stillness for prayer either. Possessions or no possessions, families or not, every day we are challenged to find the quiet places inside. For these places of perfect understanding are not something we either have or have not but are places in ourselves that we must find every day. Silence is not merely the absence of sound but the truth that is in all sound. Monks or nuns still find plenty of noise in their minds or from members of their community that distracts their heart's prayer. Silence is the pure sound found inside the noise we live with both inside us and outside in the world. When we listen for the silence in every noise we find room for prayer.

Life is full of human struggles needing to be filled with silence through prayer. The monastery is not an escape from life's struggles but simply a place to remember to attach prayer to every struggle, so that the presence of the unsounded is always with us.

The monastery with or without walls is a place where we can find the heartfelt prayer that takes us to the silence inside. In the monastery no difficulty or distraction is more powerful than prayer. No matter how loud or how painful life's moments may seem, prayer can lead us to the intimate space that is always more available and much greater.

Every monastery can provide at best a shelter for prayer and for learning the ways of silence. The quiet places inside us discover that obstacles to the silence are not enemies to battle with but are before us as an invitation. Each barrier to silence is given to us to help forgive and heal so that more of life will be included in the silence, more of our soul returned to our awareness. We are given noise to heal so that the silence can be sung again, the notes more loudly and clearly lifting our hearts. Every obstacle is here for us, for prayer, to help restore the natural music of silence, so that the world once again can be a great cathedral of silence.

———

In their search for the silence, monks and mystics through the ages have learned to go into the silence not by leaving the noise of the world but by discovering the pure sound in the noisy world we live in. Prayer can help uncover the silence not by giving up or shying away from life but by awakening us to life in all its intensity, its playful and joyous beauty.

The search is in each prayer, for every prayer is challenged by the noise inside us. Prayer is challenged whether it is expected of us or spontaneously pouring from our domain of silence toward greater silence. Every prayer comes from a discipline of tradition or a discipline of opening the heart. At one time or another, the desire for a prayerful life reaches the cliffs of disappointment in everyone. Then it is up to each of us to decide whether our heartful prayer ends and we turn back, or we listen for a new prayer, one of deepening desire. Every day we are challenged to be present for prayer, for the silence. Every day, through every prayer, the search continues.

———

Prayer gives the silence, which is the very clear song that is simple, full of devotion, full of itself, in nature, in everyone. The notes of the silence lift every bird and are perfect for every heart, one note at a time.

If any prayerful life leads us to describe the silence as being something other than an immense love, then we are describing something other than the silence.

————

Work

The search for silence includes our work. Like prayer, work challenges the monk or mystic in everyone. When the monk gives up everything and enters the monastery he still has to work. Every day the monastic life inside us is called to find a new relationship with our work. Each day is either routine or full of life depending upon our relationship to the silence. Do we find creativity, play, and meaning in our work or do we work simply to get through another day? Whether supporting our families or a spiritual community we all work. Do we go to work for survival, for future rewards like vacations, or for some special status? Work can be an opportunity to gain knowledge of the silence, to discover the free parts of us available for silence no matter how busy we are. Work can teach us how to rely on the hidden harmony during the most pressure-filled times, the moments of decisions. Inside the walls of the most sacred monastery there are no easy solutions to the mystery of our relationship to work. There is, however, the old tradition of men and women looking for work's true meaning. The search for silence calls us to be present physically, mentally, emotionally. Work expands our interior life, opening us again and again to the silent world inside us. During work, the silence can help us relax and come forth with more of our being, our creativity, our inner knowing. Work can be part of our search for inspiration in every aspect of life including how we make a living.

Community

The search for silence continues in our relationships with our partner and community, in how we relate to the "other" in all of life. Wholeness for everyone includes solitude and meaningful relationships. The monk or nun inside us searches for silence in genuine relationships that add to the silence in each person instead of distract. Whether with a spiritual community or with a partner, relationships can either expand our prayerful life or keep us busy and away from ourselves. Whether with a community or with a partner, we agree to surrender our independence and let go of some of our self-importance. We end up thankful for the opportunity. Or sometimes we surrender unconsciously from habit or weakness and later often feel guilty and resentful. To become conscious of the silence is to become more conscious and whole in all our relationships.

Relationships challenge us to find love's silence. Do we let each other inside our hearts and how far? What is intimacy other than shared silence? Are we aware that with each person we receive comes the presence of silence that is within them? Our efforts in creating a true relationship calls for forgiveness of the differences we may have or the annoyances that occur. Forgiveness is central to every monastery, with or without walls. The search for silence is often centered around our partners, families, spiritual community. These are the most visible presence of the silence. They are the carriers of the love of the silence, alive, breathing, taking risks in the same room with us.

Monks and mystics in monasteries in the desert, remote valleys and mountaintops, the monk or mystic inside us, in cities and the countryside, among every class of people, are challenged today by the same cry and search for silence. Modern technology has made the earth increasingly smaller, and with the fast pace to modern life, each area of silence left is increasingly threatened. We search for the inner quiet that will free us from the stressful noise, that will unify the many voices we carry inside. We search for the intimate stillness that will liberate us to physically change the noise we live with. And we search for the silence that will help us to rise above the noise around us that we cannot change. We cry and search for the silence that will bring us together with our partners, families, and communities. We search for the unsounded wonder that will inspire us to find life's meaning. We want to find the silent places within us where love's presence can find refuge and grow in our lives.

CHAPTER TWO

MEDITATION

We come to know the silence reaching all the way to the stars and beyond as we grow to know the intimate stillness in the little details of our day. The silence shows that the light of the stars and the light inside us are made of the same love as we open ourselves to receive the beauty.

Meditation opens our lives, empties our minds, and prepares our bodies and emotions for the silence. Meditation shows us that the intimate details of life are full of silence. More than a technique, more than repeating a certain phrase, meditation is a way to become silent, a way to encourage silence to become a part of us.

Meditation is more than what we normally call meditation. It includes the moments before and after sitting in meditation. It is what we feel in our bodies when we practice yoga or exercise. It helps us stay focused through life's bends and turns no matter where we go or are led to.

In the West, meditation comes with difficulty because the Western mind is trained to be busy and rewarded for being analytic, critical, and productive. In the East, meditation comes naturally because the Eastern mind appreciates a life of simply being and realizes that the cycle of time and timelessness is central to every soul.

In the East, meditation is part of the reality of being one soul in a country crowded with millions. Value is placed on finding one's place here and now and in eternity. Meditation is part of life where fear is driven away by a loving God. Devotion to love in the silence takes the place of devotion to things. Life in the silence is respected and sought after by many beings.

In the West, meditation requires us to more consciously take the time to become attuned to the silence. Whether we meditate in our rooms with a simple altar of candles and flowers or in church during holy mass, we are taking the time to appreciate the quiet presence. Whether we rest in nature or listen to sacred music, we are allowing our soul to feel safe, to breathe and relax in the intimate union. Whether we actively pray or are still, alone or in a group, we are finding our soul's own way of being. And our meditation changes as we hear and feel the needs of our soul differently. We practice meditation to create more space for our soul to be present.

Through meditation, unnecessary thoughts can be recognized as such, slowed down, and eventually stopped. The mind can safely rest in the arms of the silence where life's vulnerability is accepted, loved, and cared for. Meditation is a daily "diet" of silence where the mind joins the heart to nourish us. Meditation restores trust, melting our will into the will of the silence. Meditation is like drinking from the source, the well of silence inside, unifying our soul with the vast stillness.

Meditation relieves the burdens we carry in our minds, our emotions, our bodies, our relationships. When experienced, the peace of our soul affects every part of life. Meditation is not a time to put aside our cares but to listen more consciously for the silence in our everyday lives. Meditation is the silence inside us listening to the great vast stillness.

Order is restored. Balance is achieved. The resonance in the silence lifts our entire being.

Meditation is opening the window so that the silence can be with us directly. In meditation the words of the unvoiced world can be heard. The presence of the silence can be seen and felt. The will of the unchanging love inside us can be known.

As we offer more of ourselves to the great love in the silence, our minds have less to think about and worry over. Our thoughts focus more directly on whatever concerns us, our emotions are less overwhelming and more easily accepted. Meditation each day comes naturally as our minds become empty, available for the silence. Meditation attunes our minds to the frequency of love's stillness, the love our souls are calling for.

The souls who have the courage to meditate put themselves into the silence as an empty bowl. And of course the perfect stillness fills the bowl and rushes over the rim as well.

Meditation teaches us to find a place for the unnecessary thoughts that remain in the way. The thoughts that wander in and out of our consciousness, the thoughts that repeat themselves with nowhere to go, are what we create to lessen the intensity of the silence and its sweetness. They are really nothing. But as long as we are busy thinking, our thoughts will prevent the beautiful stillness from pouring into our soul. We are not meditating. We are being busy in the midst of the overwhelming simplicity that is ready to join us. Give our thoughts less attention. Meditation is not merely an exercise of the mind, but is also an expression of our body's hunger for the divine, our connection with the perfect quietude. Sitting with our desire for love we cannot help but feel how close the intimacy of the silence is to us.

Every time we meditate we stop wherever we are and feel once again the silence about us, within us. Meditation is remembering again and again that we live in the quiet harmony, our lives are clothed in the silence. Meditation is the practice of being present.

Once we learn how to stop the unnecessary thoughts and enter the simple presence, we can more easily recognize the silence as being with us and leading us. Many people do not feel their own inner guidance because they do not have a feeling for the presence of silence within them. Meditation builds this place of simplicity within so that we can discern the voice that guides us and that comes from the authentic silence, our ground of being. We learn to discern this voice from the noise we live with. Finding the "true voice" comes from our practice of meditation. Our true voice is the one that is not reacting out of fear but is gently moving us closer to the love in the silence. Our true voice speaks for our inner-most being instead of echoing the loudest voices around us. This voice has a tone and melody that those who hear can feel and trust as true.

Meditation is to listen again and again. Meditation is the time to ask for the silence to take us on the journey we have always desired. These are the times to practice listening to what our soul really yearns for. Meditation is the time to tell the uncreated being what we want and ask the silence for what is best for us. The dialogues that we have in meditation, the dialogue between our mind and our soul, our heart and the great heart in the silence, help us to find the one voice, the truth for our lives. Meditation is the time when the silence gives witness to what we are thinking about, what we are worrying over, what we are seeking, and what our souls are really here for. Meditation is the time when the perfect love within us separates the noise in our hearts from the pure desire that is in us. Through meditation we can be relieved of our compulsion to need so many little comforts because the silence brings us the real comfort. We are relieved of our daily little desperations because the perfect quiet pacifies our inner fears. We become less busy as we feel how much the silence is with us, living and working for us in our lives.

There are no unfailing techniques for meditation. Meditation is more than a question of how long or short we sit in the stillness, more than how concentrated or divided our attention is. These are the moments in which a very personal relationship is developing. Meditation is the courtship, the romance, and eventually the marriage where we are one with the silence and no longer resist it possessing us.

The joy and happiness of marriage experienced on earth is only a small symbol of the intense light and great love for us in our union with the silence. Meditation is how we develop this relationship. This is why we meditate in the most beautiful places, to feel the beauty in the silence. This is why we meditate where it is most peaceful so that we can enter the peace that is in the stillness. Every meditation is another experience with the Intimate Being. We meditate until our life is full of nothing less than love's beautiful intimacy.

This relationship calls us to the present again and again. Instead of looking backward or forward, meditation helps bring us to the point where there are just the silence and our feelings. Our hearts find their sacred place as we practice listening, affirming our place in the hidden life. There are no distractions that can deny us love's victory in the silence. Our desire for the love in the silence is enough to give us a life full of love's many qualities.

Meditation is reconnecting, simply remembering our soul's existence. The simple harmony is wherever we are, in whatever we are doing. Each moment of meditation sets us once again in the space of infinite creation, reminding us that our lives are full of divine possibilities.

TRUTH OF BEING

Meditation leads to a life full of the truth of being rather than to the truth that is measured, tested, and diagnosed. Our beingness can influence any measure, any test, any diagnosis. Meditation leads to the truth of being that values not so much what we do and what we have, but who we are. It encourages us to be ourselves instead of trying to be something different. The truth of our being gives the silence, our inner world, the monk and mystic inside us a place to prevail. Our accomplishments and successes are seen not more or less important than what they are. Our struggles, worries, challenges, and joys are aspects of life in the vast stillness. Meditation gives us the self-confidence to resist the promises and temptations of the world and yield instead to the love in the silence.

The truth of simply being can radically change the way we live and eventually our entire culture. As people find that the love in the silence is more satisfying than their drive for status and importance, they begin to question their life-style and the fast pace of living. Their values of being and caring begin to supersede their values of possessing and doing. Meditation is leading many people to a life full of silence. It is helping them to realize that they need fewer things to consume and less hectic schedules.

Meditation leads us to question our fears of scarcity and loneliness and to ask again what will bring us lasting happiness. There are many life-styles advertized and pro- moted. Life is full of pressures to go one way and then another in our work and relationships, in our thoughts and feelings. Meditation helps us reside within the silence in ourselves where we can sort out what is true and what appeals to our fears. The truth of being needs no convincing. There are no arguments, no claims, no promises necessary. The silence inside us resonates with truth and recognizes love when it is with us. The truth of being recognizes that life is simple, and when it is not we know that we are out of touch with the silence.

A life that is true not only is self-serving but also serves others. The quality of life of those around us is part of our own quality of life. We have no need to make some people wrong and others right; we shouldn't embrace those who are close to us while ignoring the cries of others who are farther away. The silence is the home for everyone. Our meditation helps us find the love in the quiet everywhere, in everyone we meet. This love brings us together. We want to give more of ourselves to the silent being as we naturally find ourselves wanting to give more to others.

Many ask, "If truth is so easy to understand, why is it so difficult to live the truth?" It lies within our being in the silence. Our relationship with the silence makes it possible for our understanding to become a way of life. As we give ourselves to the silence we find ourselves giving more to everyone, in many daily situations. As we learn to receive more from the silence, we learn to receive more in all kinds of situations. And every time we give and receive, we find more truth to live from. Giving and receiving are found to be one in the same. They are both possible when we feel the support of the silence.

Truth of being can have a profound impact on our lives. The more we give the more expanded we feel. The more expanded we become the more we can receive the love in the silence to give even more. The truth of friendship comes as we make a special effort for our friends. The truth of our wealth comes when we hold onto less of what we have and discover how much we have to give. The truth of love comes in our giving as much love as we have to give and learning to depend upon the source of love, the silence, for everything. Our fears of loneliness, scarcity, emptiness, are the roots of our resistance to give. In giving we prove our fears are empty.

The truth of being in the silence becomes evident the more we give ourselves to the quiet presence. In all occasions the more we give of ourselves the more silence we have to give from. This is why the saints were always giving. They found the compassion that held them close to others in the stillness. They lived so close to the silence that giving was a natural thing to do. The truth of being requires us to give because there is so much truth. Without giving there would be no room for the truth to be inside us. We cannot hold onto our fears and the truth simultaneously. The love in and of the silence helps us to give in every part of our lives, especially in those parts where we are afraid and do not want to give. It is this perfect love that gives us an ever fresh capacity to let go of fears.

When we give to others, we are giving to the silence within them. Whenever we are giving, we are connecting souls and hearts in the silence. Everywhere we give we are supporting the love in the seen and unseen realms. This is why giving is so important. Meditation helps us to feel the support of the invisible worlds. Daily life is full of opportunities to give back to love in all dimensions.

Today most education is about how to do or produce something. It teaches us very little about the truth of being. Education helps us develop skills of many kinds. The truth of being helps us develop our ability to lead whole lives, to have satisfying relationships, work, and feelings about ourselves. In order for education to include truth, it would have to teach us about the silence and about taking risks to develop a relationship with the unknown, which is our true source of security and intimacy. If education were full of truth, it would teach the ways of love and compassion, how to give and serve in many different situations. Imagine if our children were taught how to risk, give, love, and turn to the silence within them for the resources to know themselves and others more. True education would include the presence of stillness. True education would be more than history, mathematics, and science. It would teach us how to restore the quiet in our lives where the truth of simply being is readily available.

SIMPLE WORDS

Meditation that leads us to a life of simply being also leads us to a life of fewer words, each with greater meaning.

There are words that fill the air with noise for a few moments and there are simple words that come out of the silence and have something to say. There are words that quickly fall to the ground and disappear because they have nothing, are nothing, being only sounds with no substance. And there are the few chosen words that unite souls in the silence. Words that have some value always speak for the silence, represent the silence, and carry the clear song that the silence sings. Words that are true are never self-seeking but seek the silence in others to care for or rest within.

The words worthy of being spoken are those that the silence gives to us to share. This is why meditation is so important. The words that come from the quiet place within us speak less of fear and more of love's opportunities. These words are almost always of love, because love is the essence of the unsounded presence and love leads to service. Words that last are words that sweeten. These words have no self-importance or selfishness, because they know that every word offered to another person goes to the silence in each of us. True words are simple. They are the flesh of the silence. Our meditation leads us to the words that have the right tone and melody, the simple words that are perfect for expressing love in a way that can be received. Meditation helps us reach into our interior silence for those words that are sacred and that can deeply touch another human being.

After we have said all that we need to say, the silence can begin to speak. In us, through us, the true presence will never leave our mouths dry for the right word to quench our thirst.

The questions remain: How do we find the right words, the words rooted in the silence? How can our words be filled with substance so that they can represent the great stillness?

Through meditation we can learn how to speak from our place of silence. Here, only the words of the silence, the spiritual love, the giving thoughts, enter our mouths. Daily meditation creates for us this place of stillness inside to live and speak from.

Words of substance are true. They are more than honest. Honesty can originate from a desire to get even, to hurt, or to influence someone. Honesty can be used to impose our feelings and will over the feelings and will of others. Each of us has had someone say to us, "I'm just being honest with you." Meanwhile our feelings are hurt and the situation is anything but clear or complete. Honesty that comes from caring, wanting to love, and sincerely serving another being is filled with the words that are more than honest, they are true.

By listening to our words, we gradually recognize that the silence inside us is speaking. Are our words to impress others or to serve them? Are our words guarded and protected or open and loving? Are our words for selfish purposes or for purposes of the perfect harmony, to love and to honor whom we are speaking with? Are our words ours, like a possession, or are they for whoever wants to receive them?

———

When our words are speaking for the silence, we are listening to the silence, asking for the right words to come. The language of the silence is very conscious, clear, and precise. More is said with fewer words. The words produce no fear. The words of the silence communicate love and ready each heart to receive. The world needs fewer words, each with more meaning and love. Our words can be the words of the angels full of the presence of sacredness.

———

THE MONASTERY

Meditation in the monastery is a constant practice. The life of prayer, work, and spiritual community are all part of meditation. Meditation focuses on everyday experiences, leading meditators to experience more of the great love in the silence. The monk or nun inside us has the opportunity to be just as constant as those living in monasteries. Through our meditation our ordinary lives are woven into the perfect stillness, and the stillness weaves our lives into love's presence.

The small number of active monasteries and other silent refuges where monks, nuns, and mystics live is not enough to hold the presence of silence for the world. We all must share this responsibility. Silence, the truth of being, and the simple words that represent the love in the silence must not disappear, because the love in our homes, workplaces, and places of healing would also disappear. Practicing meditation is how we build up the quiet places in ourselves and in our relationships and communities. Practicing meditation is how we preserve and increase our interior life, safeguarding the silence, our being, the power of our words. Practicing meditation is what brings our words and actions back to the source, our inner place of substance. Meditation creates more space in life for the soul and less space for words and actions empty of meaning. Meditation allows us to look upon the beauty of the world so that our lives reflect this beauty. Meditation leads us to the presence of silence, heaven's awareness for us to live in.

The monastery without walls is made up of people everywhere, who meditate, celebrate the presence of silence, and enjoy a life of simply being. In the monastery without walls we are called to affirm the truth of being. Spiritual values prevail over material values. Fewer words are spoken and those that are spoken are fuller of love's presence, the simple words that come from the silence. We are challenged to find our true life in the silence instead of continuously reacting to the noise around us. Meditation is the simple invitation for the quiet presence to be with us, the discovery of silence in every relationship, every part of life.

CHAPTER THREE

PRAYER

Prayer is the language of the silence. As our appreciation of the silence is disappearing so is our appreciation of prayer. Prayer is perhaps the first language, the only language known in every culture. Prayer is the language that the silence is intimate with. It is the language of the heart. Everyday words are empty until they are used in prayer and then they become full of the substance of silence. It is as if through prayer each word is held and delivered into the vast quiet. Prayer takes the words from our heart and brings them to the divine heart in the silence. The purpose of prayer is the experience of prayer itself and not necessarily the results we are praying for.

———————

Prayer is the language given by the unvoiced world to lead us to the pathways and meadows of the pure garden in the silence. Ordinary life is filled with silence through the experience of prayer. Each prayer is like a guided walk into the quiet garden. This garden is where we can express our love fully. With every prayer more light of the garden appears in the eyes and the heart. With each visit another part of our lives is planted in the silent garden and we return more connected to eternity. This is why monks and mystics live with such little fear during their brief time on earth. Prayer after prayer they come back with their pockets full of seeds from the perfect garden to nourish their soul and to make life a garden just as whole and pure.

Prayer leads us into the silence for every need, bringing our lives into the quiet world where everything is whole and well. And of course each time we return from the quiet wonder our hands and pockets are filled with wholeness and wellness. But the success of our prayer is not in what we return with but in how close are we willing to be to the heart of the silence. Our success comes not from the words used but in how much of our mind, heart, and being are put into the words. The more we pray the more we find the garden's perfect calm and care.

Although there are many types of prayer, most begin with our present vulnerability. Prayer naturally takes our insecure physical lives, which are full of the upset from everyday noise, into the secure place of stillness. Each word begun on the edge of our vulnerability is taken to new boundaries, where the soul rests in the silence. Prayer can take us immediately beyond the words where there are only answers, only oneness. With prayer the words are heard even before they are spoken. Through prayer the silence receives us until we feel understood. The silence is the one place that receives us completely. Once this is experienced, we find less need to struggle so much to prove ourselves, to convince others we are right, or to search for someone special who understands us. Each prayer takes us to deeper understanding and acceptance of ourselves and others. Each prayer sheds more light on the pathway into the silence.

PRAYER FOR OURSELVES

Prayer for ourselves takes our everyday life, our joys and problems, into the peaceful presence of the stillness. Prayer takes the parts of our lives that feel overwhelmed and heavy to where there is no weight. The fragmented parts of our lives are brought back into the love of the silence. This is why people of diverse backgrounds and cultures who are introduced to the mysteries of prayer often make a life full of prayer. Each prayer is our personal route through the physical world into the quiet realms. If we begin to pray when we feel blocked and immovable, prayer opens the way for the quiet to wash into our lives and remove the obstacles by its sheer magnitude. The power of prayer is in the strength of the hidden harmony. As our hearts open to the immense heart of the silence, the power of prayer becomes limitless. The quality of our prayer grows with our awareness of love's prayerful presence.

Daily prayer takes us back to the great heart of the silence, which receives us completely. Love attends to every concern, every cry, as no friend or partner could. The prayer for ourselves slowly changes our perception of who we are. If through prayer we can feel the great heart of the silence, who can say where this love begins and ends? Who can say what is our heart and what is the heart of the silence? Through our prayers the world of the stillness expands in us. And we become more conscious of the heart at the center. Our prayers lead us repeatedly to ask, "Can we receive the intense light and gentle tenderness the silence has to offer?"

PRAYER FOR OTHERS

Prayer for others invites the quiet presence to be physically closer to them. Prayer for others not only reinforces the presence of love for those we pray for, but also connects the silence in us with the silence in them. Prayer for others affirms how much we are connected with all beings. Each prayer reminds us that in the great stillness we are not separate. Every prayer for another communicates to that person that he or she has a soul and is part of the perfect silence. Prayer helps the conscious mind to let go and surrender to more of the invisible harmony that carries us. Prayer for others works as if we are opening many direct channels into the silence. Love in the silence not only moves toward those we pray for, but also reflects and therefore returns to us the love we have given. Each prayer for others expands our own being, for we receive the silence through them. They become part of our spiritual body. Together we are more in the silence than if just by ourselves.

During the prayer for ourselves we can feel the calming and the lessening of our separations. But during the prayer for others we are often preoccupied with having results. Simply connecting with the silence in others and loving them through prayer are not enough. We want results. We think the important thing is not the prayer itself but the response. We are tempted to judge the silence and the prayer by what physical results they can produce. But from the point of view of the silence the important thing is not that the prayer is answered but that it is said. Our need for evidence of the power of the silence comes from our fear that we are alone and no special presence is with us. It is hard to believe there is a great presence holding the stillness and the world together. So we pray, open our eyes, and wonder if our prayers really work. And often the answers come as quickly as this. More often, however, the physical challenges we encounter are not meant to be solved so easily but are here to pull us to the depths of prayer and the possible depths of being in these quiet-filled places.

Silence and prayer are like two best friends who take each other on all kinds of journeys. Through prayer we find the hidden rooms and gardens of silence within us. Through prayer we pierce through the surface of other people's lives and current troubles, to the place of

*stillness within them. Our prayer for others reminds us
of the inner resources we have within. Prayer continues to increase our faith in love's presence, always
taking us to new areas of exploration in the oneness.*

PRAYER IN CRISES

Prayer in crises can be like a desperate plunge into the
silence. Although such prayer obtains results, the soul is not
prepared to receive all of the silence's peace. The prayerful
life prepares us to live in the intense light and love hidden in
the stillness. Our desperate attempts are heard and re-
sponded to. But our daily prayer builds a much stronger and
clearer relationship with the silence. We know exactly how
much more we need the silence, how much we can be within
the quiet presence, and how much we are already familiar
with it. Prayer that only tests the silence yields limited proof
of the great presence. However, prayer in crises can also
bring us very close to the intimate space. Such prayer is not
necessarily less valuable. Our tests can be a door that opens
onto a new prayerful life after decades of being closed. After
the crisis is over, we can proceed with daily prayer for
ourselves and for others. Prayer in crises can have a great
impact on the emergency as more energy than usual is being
focused and more peace is being channeled into the conflicts.

TRADITIONAL AND REPETITIVE PRAYER

Traditional prayer has a history, an established path into
the silence. The Shema in Judaism, the Lord's Prayer in
Christianity, the prayer for all beings in Buddhism, the many
prayers in Hinduism and other religions; each has a path
tread by millions into the stillness. The path is well marked
by these prayers. But each prayer can simply be part of the
crowd making the silence less than fresh and alive for each
soul praying. The well-established prayers touch the silence
when they are said without sincerity, but each person's own

involvement is important to add to the silence, to support the many dimensions and realms of love. For some people, traditional prayers have become words with little substance. These people sometimes leave organized religion and search elsewhere. However, the problem is not the prayers but the way they are taught, said, and experienced.

Some traditional prayers serve specific purposes. For example the rosary helps develop a relationship with God as our Mother. Said again and again, the rosary creates a close bond between the silence and all the feminine aspects of God. The soul who opens to God as Mother develops a special intimacy with the Divine Mother, the kind of relationship we wish we could have had with our biological mother who was too human to be divine. It is through the daily repetition of the rosary that this relationship blooms into certainty. Repetitive prayer opens the quiet presence within us again and again until the strength of the prayer is solidly with us. We have the opportunity to put more of our being into the prayer each time it is said. Repetitive prayer becomes a mantra that keeps resonating so that eventually the consciousness of every cell is being touched. Repetitive prayer is really never the same from one time to the next, because we are always feeling different and the silence is new each time we pray. Every prayer that is used over and over again finds more union with the silence if said each time as though it were the first and only time.

Prayer that goes into the perfect stillness intending to stay finds a home there and never leaves us. Prayer that is filled with desire goes into the silence and returns full of peace and acceptance. But prayer that is quick and automatic goes to the edge of the great quiet and no farther. The silence is too alive, too real for the empty words to go to its heart. It is the many messengers and servants of the silent realms who take every prayer to the great heart to be received. Because of the unlimited love in the silence, all prayer is heard. Prayer that begins in our depths and takes as much of our being with it as possible, travels easily and lands in the depths of the immense being of the silence.

PRAYER FOR CLEARING THE HEART

Whether for ourselves or for others, in crises or as a religious tradition, all prayers are for clearing the heart. Through prayer we reach into the silence for the love that soothes each hurt, each pain. Through prayer we can return a crowded life of noise to the clear heart of silence. In prayer our body is occupied by the peace. It is this peace that restores our well-being, our emotions. It is this peace that gives us a deeper understanding of our relationship to the silence. The obstacles in our heart, our hurts and disappointments, are healed with prayer's peacefulness. It is prayer that reminds us that we are much more than our physical selves, more than our relationships, more than our thoughts and emotions. Prayers remind us of our endless connection in the lucid stillness.

It is never too late to clear our hearts through prayer. Whether someone has moved away or has died, does not speak to us or will not stop fighting with us, one soul's prayer can heal any relationship. In prayer there is no distance. Whether someone has moved a thousand miles away or has died and passed over to the other side, prayer takes us into the fullness of the stillness where we are still connected with their essence. And in this connection, inviting the peace of prayer always has value. As we make peace, the silence in the other person feels it, knows it. We only have to surrender to the peace. The person may persist in being angry. The distance between us may seem the same. But the peace of our prayer touches the silence in that person. We cannot change others against their will, but through clearing our hearts our prayer keeps love next to them, keeps the door open the moment they want to change. Prayer offers the best of ourselves and the silence to every situation.

PRAYER OF FORGIVENESS

In many ways all prayer is an act of forgiveness. Opening to prayer invites the natural forgiveness of the great quiet. Forgiveness is part of the very fabric of the silence. Forgiveness practiced regularly and sincerely promises to keep us close to the simple presence. Prayer helps us forgive by opening our heart to the love of the silence, filling our hurt and disappointment with the silent peace. Every disturbance to us has created a disturbance in the silence and can be settled with simple forgiveness. Great acts of forgiveness come from the heart of the silence and strengthen the invisible harmony everywhere, in everyone. Prayer helps us to live a life of forgiveness by reminding us that we are more than our thoughts and emotions, that we can forgive from the place of silence that is always within us.

Forgiveness is the act of giving to a situation instead of waiting for someone else to take the first step. Forgiveness is drawing upon the heart of love, the peace of prayer, the oneness in each other to soothe the disturbance that is occupying our thoughts. Forgiveness is celebrating love instead of being a victim of love's wounds. Prayers of forgiveness provide a path that leads us away from hurt and disappointment to the presence of silence. Forgiveness is what we discover when we draw from the well of love in the gentle stillness. Forgiveness includes the understanding, the compassion, the truth, and the qualities of silence we find in prayer, ourselves. Prayer brings peace to lives in need of forgiveness. We are bringing love. Forgiveness puts our heart in alignment with the sacred heart in the intimate quiet. And when we cannot forgive, when we feel so wronged that forgiveness is impossible, prayer brings us to the heart that is greater than our own and is the source of all forgiveness. Prayer and every act of forgiveness remain interconnected, inseparable.

Forgiveness for all the small details that seem to distract us puts us back on the path of no distractions.

Forgiveness for all the hardness we experience in ourselves and others soon introduces us to the softness in everyone, the soft silence, the tender love. Forgiveness for our confusion in life, our selfishness, our ever-persistent fears, for when we hurt others, slowly returns us to the deep currents of compassionate understanding and provides for all our needs. The silence greets our prayer with perfect forgiveness.

Forgiveness is the foundation for life in the monastery. If monks or nuns do not forgive the members of their communities for the little ways they have been hurt, how do they expect to feel the great unifying forgiveness of the silence? Each of us is called to shape each prayer carefully so that forgiveness is in the very essence of our words, full of the humility that makes prayer effective for peaceful daily living.

PRAYER OF INNOCENCE

Forgiveness is like the skin of the silence. Inside the skin of the silence we discover innocence. Forgiveness and innocence and prayer are inseparable. One is not known without the other. And with forgiveness, innocence is more present. Our innocence makes it is easier to be more forgiving. Monks and mystics feel forgiveness and innocence living so intimately with the kind attentions they find in the vast stillness.

Each moment in the perfect quiet is like a dip into the clear water of innocence. The silence is the water that washes and refreshes us. The still ocean is felt and enjoyed one instant at a time. We are soothed in its presence. The silence restores our innocence. Each experience of prayer into the peaceful quiet returns with renewed innocence.

Children with their naturalness and many older people in their simplicity find their way into the silence to pray. Their innocence makes prayer casual, a normal part of life. As we rediscover prayer, our original innocence comes just as simply. We can easily see the innocence of children and older people. The test is to see the innocence of those who are somewhere in between. Regardless of our mistakes, we have more innocence at the beginning and the end of life because the silence is naturally closer. The silence is the bearer of innocence no matter what the current season of our life is. As prayer returns us to the qualities of being in the silence, our innocence is strengthened, and our judgment; our worries over success and failure, our drive to be happy, and our sorrows become less intense. Every prayer we make into the intimate awareness helps restore our hearts, clear our paths, opening us again to innocence. The qualities of peacefulness, gentleness, solitude and quiet in the silence all serve to build our innocence.

Living close to the silence we frequently face the question of where innocence begins and where it ends. The more we pray, the more we see how human we really are. Prayer is what brings new energy for forgiveness and renewed innocence to all we see. An intense life of prayer can only lead us to ask, "What parts of ourselves are innocent and what parts are not?" If we lived in the silence, we would answer this question differently than if we lived only to survive in today's noisy world. The loss of innocence today is directly related to the loss of silence. Children are pushed and hurried to leave childhood. There is little silence for older people to retire in and learn to enjoy. Prayer, our life in the perfect quiet, keeps us forever innocent, young at heart, and not afraid to become old.

As the prayerful life clears our heart, bringing forgiveness and innocence, we are inclined to pray for the small, everyday things that make life enjoyable and the large, important things like new relationships, work, and healing that makes us happy. We approach the great love as if it is naturally ours. Monks and mystics like Saint Francis, for example, develop an almost childlike relationship with life in how they take it for granted, cherishing it without being afraid of losing it. The silence has become the secret friend they miss from childhood. Through prayer, the stillness returns them to the innocent joy and wonder they left behind. Their lives teach us that it is not so much a question of what to pray for but a question of how much are we willing to receive.

THE MONASTERY

As life in the world can become superficial because of the avoidance of silence, life in the monastery can become callous without a prayerful life that brings forgiveness and innocence. Without love, prayer is only words. And silence is merely the absence of noise.

The monk or mystic inside us depends on the monastery without walls as a place of prayer and forgiveness. Daily prayer gently allows forgiveness for all hurts, particularly those hurts that are hard to forgive. Prayers for forgiving the little hurts make it easier to open to the prayers that forgive the seemingly unforgivable ones.

The life of forgiveness and innocence is connected intimately with prayer and our experience of the simple quiet. Our need for forgiveness keeps us close to the shared silence with our partners and community. Our innocence keeps us close to our companions in the stillness. The presence of prayer restores our belief in the invisible. Each prayer as a wrapping around peace helps us enjoy the everlasting sweetness of the fruits of the silence.

Each prayer weaves the thread of forgiveness and innocence into another part of our being. Where worldly life is an evasion of silence, the monastic part of us provides the quiet freedom where our physical life and prayer are woven into the sacred.

CHAPTER FOUR

DAILY LIFE IN THE SILENCE

Our way into love's presence finds increasing substance in daily life as we include the silence. It is through being aware of the silent presence about us, feeling the love within us, and practicing simply being in the midst of what we are doing that life becomes centered and full of moments of golden stillness. Activities such as preparing meals, eating, working, cleaning, shopping, taking care of children, attending meetings, bathing, and taking walks offer moments to explore new dimensions of the silence. These are the moments of silence that are part of everyday reality, but we are usually too busy to notice them or haven't learned how to appreciate them.

Daily life is to convert to the silence, so that love's presence is increasingly in everything we do. When our goal is a sacred life, the ordinary moments can be love's moments, silent lessons in loving the details of life. With everything we do we have inside a way of being that includes awareness and attunement with our relationship with the silence. It seems that no matter what we are doing, we can be focused, feeling, being present, so the silence is included. Whether we are working at our jobs or caring for children, cleaning the house or chatting with a friend, our attention can wander from one thing to another or we can be more involved with all our senses, paying attention to our inner world, appreciating the world of oneness that is always with us. Everything we do has an inner experience. And each experience is created out of the unfolding silence inside us.

We can uncover the secrets of the silence as we accept the challenges to participate, age, and grow wise in love's awareness. Every activity and relationship offers the unique presence of silence. Life is one stage after another, each containing a vast unspoken treasure. From infancy to old age, from sickness to health, from childhood to parenthood, from being single to being a partner to being single again, every stage of life reflects different aspects of our relationship to the silence.

We develop this relationship by changing our perception, remembering the world of silence that is within us. The silence is always a part of us. So instead of being preoccupied about getting to the next stage of life, we should take the time to enjoy the present stages, reflect, and open to what is happening now. Our meditations and prayers can expand our awareness of life by taking our everyday activities into the truth of being. Whatever season of life we are in, whether the season seems to last forever or disappear too quickly, its meaning broadens when the silence is included. It is not how much we do in life that ultimately satisfies but how much we experience life that makes our heart grow happy and wisely.

As we value our everyday experience, we live each experience more fully. We pierce through the surface of activities to the silence that is within them. Ordinary coincidences and accidents mean more to us than they appear. Ordinary events, surprises, and sudden encounters have more meaning the closer we live to the perfect stillness. What seemingly are unrelated parts of each day become part of our one relationship with the silence. As we stay in touch with the flow of our inner life, we are not simply going from home to work to lunch to a meeting. We are in a constant reality of being. The quiet presence is carried with us, and the feelings we have are brought with us. We are taking more of our inner being consciously into every situation.

The silence is constant no matter where we are or what we are doing. Every time we become aware of the present harmony we become more conscious of the moment and what we are doing. The distracting noises we live with can alert us to seek the silence once again. Instead of reacting with anger or withdrawing, instead of complaining or not doing anything about the intrusions, our meditations and prayers can strengthen our actions to be full of love's pure sound. The perfect stillness offers a different way of listening and behaving that affects virtually every part of life. The inconveniences, detours, and obstacles we encounter can be opportunities to find the fresh experience of silence that is nearby, in the midst of all our feelings.

The silence slowly picks up every part of life if we are willing to let go and be with the quiet awareness. In our willingness to let the silence provide for our life, we become less interested in activities that dull our senses or prevent us from enjoying the peace-filled stillness. The problems of the past and worries about the future fall away from the life that is in the hands of the silence. Life is full of invitations for silence and the blessings that come out of its depths.

As we become aware of the simple oneness, we realize that there are alternatives to compulsive craving, consumption, and competition. Our lives flower in the silent garden as we learn to give and care. Love's presence in the quiet expands our being, and we find compassion for others, reacting less strongly to what appears disagreeable. Instead of hurrying, criticizing, instead of identifying with our smallest self, we permit the silence to embrace the monk or mystic inside us. We find the wholeness that includes the stillness available at the center of intense activity.

Life changes as we consciously include the silence. Walks in nature awaken our senses to the unsounded vastness. The centeredness we experience in sports can expand our contact with the stillness. Honest and caring conversations with friends give the silence a breath of fresh air. The flowers appreciated, the sunsets listened to as well as watched, the meals enjoyed after the food is gone, serve to enliven our consciousness to the value of silence. Every moment we find for being in the midst of doing, for listening between thinking and speaking, gives the silence presence in our lives. The simple quiet gives life a groundedness of being as we become rooted in silence. We are less afraid, more accepting of differences in people. The void we normally run from is filled with experiences of intimate stillness. The routines we don't enjoy and the boredom we feel beg for the quiet peacefulness. In the monastery without walls life is inspired silence. The most mundane activities are waiting for our investigation, illumination, and unification with silence.

FAMILY AND FRIENDS

A life spent with family and friends is among the greatest riches of silence. Each relationship is a relationship of shared silence. More than the words spoken and the activities done together, our relationships are an accumulation of shared silence together. Depending upon the strength of the silence between two people in a relationship, the length of silent understanding, disagreements and other noisy interruptions can either threaten the relationship or leave it untouched. Families, spouses, and best friends have the strongest bonds of shared silence. This is why when families break apart, divorces occur, and best friends no longer communicate with each other, much more than mere physical separation is taking place. The silence that was shared has been broken. The depths of hurt demonstrate how much the shared silence in these relationships has been violated.

The noise of the unhealed personalities has taken precedence over love's peace and understanding.

On the other hand, by appreciating the quiet-filled moments we share in a relationship, we can have bonds that grow and strengthen. Arguing couples can feel better about each other by taking walks together or sitting in a silent room. The noise from the conflict gives way to the silent bonds between the two. Moments of silence shared by briefly holding hands before a meal or before bedtime, or saying thank-you for the day's small but important moments, build the silence between them. Moments of silence shared together make for more honest conversation and the quiet's simple affections. Intimacy naturally flows out of a life full of silence. The simplicity finds fewer barriers to love's presence.

By appreciating the silence we are led to the unique presence of each soul in our life. Our love helps the simple quiet make a home in every loved one and makes our home in the silence that much more whole. The greater we love and appreciate each other the stronger the silence becomes. True relationships withstand the pain and conflict of disagreement because the silence holding them is greater. Times of hurt and disappointment are about more than what we usually think we are struggling with. The quiet presence in us is disturbed. We think that the other is causing the problem. But no matter who is responsible for bringing the noise to our attention, the unhealed sound in the relationship is ours. And it is the experiences of shared silence that bring harmony again. In relationships we often expect the other to make things better for us. But it is our own peace in the stillness that gives happiness. And it is the shared experiences of silence that give relationships renewed purpose, renewed faith to listen with more compassion. Just as we are called to find a new relationship with the silence when we are unhappy, partnerships and friendships that are suffering are calling for new bonds of silence. Out of these bonds come new feelings to care and appreciate each other.

Relationships break apart because the noise inside us has taken over the territory that is reserved for the silence. Two people in a relationship can reclaim the oneness by listening to the words that come out of the silence in each other. And they can continue to reclaim the union between them in every experience they enjoy together.

Healing a broken relationship takes more than adjusting to the noise in our lives, the conflicts of our personalities. Healing is building upon our lives of shared silence. Renewed moments of quiet together reaffirm the relationship and help us reclaim our own being. The times of nonbeing when we are living fearfully and separately from the simple presence are healed when someone special in our lives makes contact with us again in the silence. The love awakens the feeling of the sacred.

The people we are closest to in the stillness are often the people we most intensely feel our differences with. The perfect silence makes the noise within us sound that much louder. In our closest relationships we can struggle with each other and forgive. We can let the silent presence expose our disharmony and then let the heart of the silence help us listen to one another and bring us closer together again.

The difficulties encountered in relationships can remind us of our need for silence and, specifically, for more experiences of shared silence. Partners who are fighting, families who are not speaking, have lost contact with the sacredness of silence, the sacredness in each other. Whether eating a meal in a special restaurant, taking a bicycle ride, or sitting together for an hour in nature, we learn that relationships come back as we come back to the soul's need for the simple harmony. Friendships, marriages, and families prosper as the people involved find experiences that they enjoy together. Two people building a relationship are crystallizing in silence. This is why relationships are so fragile and so sacred. The quiet presence in each of us demands our tender respect. This is why lovers are so happy in the beginning but so challenged later on to find the same happiness. The tender peace within us and between us needs unending attention and nurturing. Love changes only inasmuch as we stop finding and enjoying the experiences of intimate silence with one another.

The challenge in relationships is to find a new relationship with the silence by letting our desire for the Intimate Being be the focus and purpose of being together. Every relationship can serve to open us to being a companion of the silence in everyone. The relationship with our parents can lead us to our spiritual parent in the silence. Relationships with our brothers, sisters, lovers, friends, employers, and landlords can direct our struggle toward the silence where the real peace, steadfast companionship, and the true answers are found. Inasmuch as we can open to how each relationship touches and stretches our emotions, thoughts, and experience, we open to discover the presence of the great intimacy. No relationship becomes our enemy. All relationships are guides to the presence of love in our lives. They give us a fresh opportunity to make peace with the noise in our lives, to uncover our souls. We make peace in our attempts at greater openness, inner honesty, and forgiveness. We appreciate the silence in each other as we risk to share new experiences together. We come together in the infinite quiet literally touching each other, instead of remaining mentally and physically apart. In the monastery without walls life takes us on a path of resheltering until we can wholly take shelter, finding our security and purpose in the silence.

There is no need to argue or fight with the noise that disturbs the silence in each other. There is no need to try to change the noise or make it somehow understood as noise. We are not here to change each other but to support each other in completely accepting the simple oneness, in life's many experiences. The more we live in our own noise, the more we are threatened by the noise from others. Every relationship can be restored, because silence once shared can never be taken apart. We may try to deny the loved shared, but the intimacy is always true and is no further than the memories of the peace-filled moments we have enjoyed together.

———

Emotions change, interests change, needs and desires change, but the love in the silence is constant. Every relationship that appreciates the silent presence lasts. The silence is the indestructible bridge between souls. In relationships the most ordinary moments, or the most exciting and difficult ones, are abundant in silence. When we are committed to unveiling the love of the stillness, tensions that could separate us give way to wonder.

———

Life in pursuit of the silent intimacy is like a conspiracy of good things that are bound to happen. The monk or mystic practices recognizing the presence of silence in each room, each garden, each walk with a friend. Always in a new disguise, the silent love calls our attention, the attention of our hearts. By building a life of shared silence we are building the essence of real community. Intimacy grows in the many ways we are with each other. Each day, every relationship, offers opportunities to be separate, to make our differences important, or to affirm love's presence in our lives. The intimacy shared in the silence gives bloom to the understanding that is more than the words spoken, the feelings enjoyed. Souls know each other as much as the silence is appreciated and celebrated within and between them. In the silence all beings live together.

Relationships and family are the substance of life in the sacred silence. Whether building a new relationship or recalling the times already together, we always have the moments of intimacy available within us. Remembering the truth and wholeness of silence shared can heal old wounds. Remembering the sacredness of shared silence can put personality conflicts into proper perspective. Making the intimacy of silence a priority in our lives removes unnecessary noise. The pure stillness is the golden fabric that holds us to each other that no distance, change in personality, or illness can pull apart.

As the silence embraces nature in all her seasons, the silence teaches us not to deny the seasons within us and in our relationships. Fall, winter, spring, and summer each have a presence in our lives. Relationships that embrace and open to fall's vulnerability, winter's emptiness, spring's hope, and summer's fullness, relationships that respect and open to their natural change of seasons, grow in wisdom and wholeness.

SEXUALITY AND CREATIVITY

In the traditional monastery detaching oneself from the world has meant detaching oneself from the physical world, including the body's needs and desires. With the emphasis on detachment, normal sexual desires can be made wrong and given more attention and importance than they would otherwise have been given. Being critical of our physical desires and needs can make life full of separation from ourselves, each other, and the peace of the silence.

The monastery without walls is more concerned with finding the pure silence than with being separate from the noise, is more concerned about a sacred life than about detaching from what may be less than sacred. Leaving the monastery walls behind means in part taking more responsibility to sort out for ourselves what is true and what is not, which experiences lead us closer to or farther from the sacredness of being.

This responsibility is felt nowhere more acutely than in our response to sexuality, where our desires and those of people we live with, the need for intimacy and truth of fidelity, all interact. It is within the temple of sexuality that the silence can be most intimate. And similarly, sexuality can be the tense behavior we use to deny and avoid love. In the closeness of the silence are love's feelings, the intensity, the purity, the frustration, and the satisfaction of our innermost being in contact with another person. Our sexuality is an experience of the most intimate stillness.

Detaching oneself from an active sexual life can lead to increased creativity. The energy is not denied but felt and directed to creative prayer, art, and other activities. But without tender respect sexual energy that is not accepted and valued becomes energy turned against ourselves and turned away from the silence.

Compulsive sex, fearful sex, and sex filled with guilt are attempts at love without feeling the support of the silence. Sexuality as only a release of tension, as reaction to a noise-filled world cuts the body off from itself and nature. The body feels separate from the temples of silence. Sexuality without participation of the silence is sexuality without love. Sexuality that is full of the silence is full of the love, the peaceful tenderness that is holy.

To live our sexuality in harmony with the silence requires us to be open to love's presence in our feelings. We do this through accepting all our feelings. As we accept our feelings, our behavior originates from choice instead of from compulsion or habit. Instead of being something denied or hidden, our sexuality is an expression of freedom, of the joy of the silence.

Our sexual feelings are not so different from life's other feelings, only sometimes they are more intensified. Gentleness, patience, desire, fulfillment, joy and laughter, excitement, and peace are all qualities of sexuality and creativity. They are also qualities of silence. If our sexuality includes moments of intimate quiet, then we will find innocence. Sexuality is creativity filled with silence in which the heart is present. Pursuing sexuality separately from the silence is a helpless act, for it shows that we are starved for the quiet's affections.

The intimate stillness is a very creative, sensual place. The love in the silence is so great that people cannot deny the experience forever or the pain if it is missing. Befriending our sexuality is to befriend the silence within us. Such a friendship includes change. Sexuality is an invitation for creativity, where love is always new and different. We are called to be sensitive to the universe of silence inside us and our partner. The silence within us, between us, is always new. Frustration with our partner is frustration with our own creativity, our relationship with the silence. We so often blame each other instead of exploring ourselves and our fears of changing our relationship with the silence. We look toward each other instead of looking toward a new awareness of the silence, our need for new openness and intimacy. Our sexuality opens us to our need for creativity, our need for the tender touches of the silence.

The monastery detaches itself from sexual activity in the understanding that love cannot be possessed. The silence is not something to hold onto once and for all. Monks and nuns live with the stillness and beside it, directing all their desires to the company of the pure stillness, which receives more of their being.

The monk or mystic inside us must do the same. Whether alone or with a partner, we must learn that love cannot be possessed. In relationships, sexuality cannot replace the need for the presence of silence. Whether alone or with a partner, we must receive the energy that springs from our depths so that we can receive the peace of the silence. In the traditional monastery, monks and nuns make a decision to devote themselves entirely to the still presence. This devotion can lift their being into beautiful realms of intimacy. They chose a life of creative selflessness so that they can be more full of the quiet and its perfect peace.

The silence invites us to the same realms of creative intimacy. Our devotion to love's presence is true whether we are alone, seeking a partner, beginning a relationship, or are in the midst of a long-term partnership. We are called to be available to love's presence in whatever season of life we are in. With our partner the love shared silently, the service we give, open us to the pure sounds of love. We are invited to give to the silence in each other as each asks to be given to. This is practicing the selflessness of the great oneness, the selflessness all monks and nuns are called to.

Sexuality in all its varieties can free the silence inside us. Sexuality can be a path to experience our creativity. Like monks and nuns, we must come to terms with the walls we maintain between the silence and us. Those who live in the traditional monastery may feel called to re-examine their commitment to see that it does not become a wall between intimacy and themselves. Is one's solitude providing more closeness of silence or cutting one off from the shared silence that comes in relationships. Similarly the monk and mystic inside us must ask whether we are avoiding solitude in our relationships? Is our sexual life giving us more experience of the sacredness or taking from it? Our lovemaking can bring down the walls between us and the silence. Or the tension and distance, the shadows in the relationship, may remain as before. The presence or absence of sexuality does not determine how close we are to the sacred harmony. Our need for expressing physical love may be our need for greater creativity. Our sexual desires may be expressing our need for more intimate relationships in general. Our sexual desires can be our desire to feel more nature, more contact with tall trees, green fields, the earth around us. Sexual desires can be a disguise for the many forms of intimacy that are missing from our lives. And our sexual desire can be no disguise at all but simply an expression of our desire for physical love. Physical love may or may not be our most sacred path of experiencing the affections of the silence. The creative, sexual energy that is so much a part of us calls for our deepest respect.

Because the silence is so very close whenever we are physically intimate, casual sexuality is really impossible.

With the silence, all love is holy. Every physical encounter brings two souls together in the silence as well as two bodies. Such intimacy is more a part of us than most people are aware or willing to admit. Every relationship in which silence is exposed and shared so intimately is sacred.

Sexuality expresses the creative joy of love's presence. It is the sparks of the silence inside us in the cosmic dance of creation.

As the monastery continues the tradition of directing sensuality to only one relationship, the direct experience of silence, those of us who live outside the cloister walls are called to the same experience of divine intimacy. With or without a partner, our sacred self thirsts for the unity in the silence. We cannot possess the love in the silence anymore than we can possess our partner. We are called to receive the love of the silence from our partner, nature, creative work and play, our prayer and meditation. The love of the vast quiet can be neither repressed nor indulged in, neither denied nor possessed, but can be simply lived with day by day.

CHILDREN

The monastery without walls includes children and celebrates them as the Intimate Being's pure creation. Children are the great teachers of the love the silence carries. Their innocence is the gift the silence brings to remind us of our own true nature. To look into the face of a child is to see the timeless face of the silence. To treasure children is to be led into the silence's unending riches.

Everyone says, "Yes, but what about my child? My child is not always so sweet and innocent. My child is . . ." Everywhere our child leads us can become an experience of the silence. Their innocence can serve to keep us open to the joys and trials that come with children.

Life is not always smooth with children. And life with children is everything but full of golden quiet. As perfect teachers our children stretch us and challenge us to find the silence everywhere as no adult teacher can do. Our children take us by the hand and lead us as much as we lead them to new experience. We can choose to struggle with and resist each experience our children bring to us or look for the peace of the silence that is present. The goal is to teach children not to avoid difficulties but create a relationship with them, so that life's disruptions and noise become opportunities to invite the peaceful silence. It is never too early or late for children to become active participants in the monastery without walls.

———

As parents, we accept our children as we would accept no one else. There is nothing they can do to destroy our love. This is an example of the intense bond of love that the silence holds for us. The love we discover for our children in all kinds of situations is a small reflection of the love for every part of our lives in the silence.

———

Children give us a great gift in all the joy and challenges they present. Our bond of silence holds us very close. Life becomes full of situations we either open to or try to control. Each time we say yes rather than no to our children, the place of silence within us is being tested. Do we answer from our lack of patience or from what we think is good for the child? Are our answers from the silence within us or from reactions to the noise in our children and in us? The search for an authentic way of being with our children brings us deeper within ourselves. We are moved to find faith, acceptance, forgiveness, compassion, gentleness, strength and much more. All these qualities are to be developed each day in the silence. As we help our children to love and accept all of themselves, we must accept and make peace with every emotion our children raise in us. As we create a life full of experience and activities worthy of their talents and being, they remind us to remain open to the aliveness of the present. There is no truer spiritual path than raising chidren.

With our hearts in their small hands, children naturally stretch our limits and challenge us to feel, accept, and discover the silence. When we give birth to our children and raise them, we are giving birth and raising much more than a physical being, more than a personality. We are giving a soul the opportunity to be in the world. Through this process our soul too has an opportunity to be reborn. In every gift of ourselves we give to our children, the silence in them grows stronger, and beings everywhere are touched with the genuineness of the love. As our children demand and confront, laugh and play in our lives, they teach us to be more ourselves in every relationship, in all of life.

TRUE NEEDS

Every monk and nun is challenged to find the difference between the real need for food, possessions, and relationships, and those needs that could be satisfied in a deeper relationship with the silence. We are similarly challenged. In addition, we must ask whether the errands we're running, the meetings we're attending, are part of our true path or are simply keeping us busy. Are the extra purchases we make and the extra food we eat part of life in the silence or are they things to occupy our attention instead of being more, living more intimately with love's presence that is with us?

Life in the monastery without walls can serve to keep our lives focused on our real needs and the sacred. Here we can better know what parts of our lives serve the silence within us and what we are doing that separates us from ourselves and the silence.

All needs can lead us first to more silence. Daily we can remind ourselves to approach the silence first so that everything we need comes so much easier. When we want shelter we can begin by taking shelter in the quiet presence. When we want food or companionship we can first nourish ourselves with the stillness and let the silence be our closest companion. As we are open, the natural order of things can answer all our needs either directly or by guiding us to the easiest solution. The more we feel our needs with the silence, the more love can reach deeper inside us, bringing the perfect shelter, the perfect food, and the perfect companion who expresses most what the silence wishes for us.

As life brings our desires to the silence, we find that we need less. The path of receiving the peaceful presence leads us to letting it fulfill us. Our continued happiness lies in the kind attentions of the silence.

Whoever has happiness needs little else. And whoever is not happy could possess the whole world and it still would not matter. The silence possesses everything for us so that we can be simply full of joy.

The sacred life means sorting out which needs are necessary and determining how time would be better spent simply being. As we become available to the affections in the silence, we find much of what we thought we needed is already given to us in the sweetness that is always present.

WORK

There is work that ensures survival and there is work that gives life meaning. The more fear influences our life, the more likely we work simply to survive. The more the simple peace fills our days, the easier it is to trust and find one's perfect work in the silence.

So often we are more attached to our job description than to what we are actually doing. It is not always the work we do that satisfies us but how close we feel to the silence in it that does. There are teachers and healers who work as if the silence has no presence in their lives. And there are field-workers and shopkeepers who live so closely to the intimate presence that nearly everyone sees a radiant love shining in their faces. The real work is to feel the silence in everything we do. We do this by being conscious of whom we are with, what we are doing, and how we are feeling. By taking care of the details in front of us, whether making phone calls or answering letters, we can become aware of the details of silence in our midst. We tune into the inner process of work, our awareness, and the needs of the moment without letting our minds wander. Awareness of the silence makes our work constantly new and stimulating. Our work is a pathway into more of the perfect quiet. This awareness makes our work constantly new and stimulating. Without a silence-filled heart, work loses its excitement no matter how prestigious and profitable it may be. If we live only for future goals, we grow further from the silence that is with us now.

If we are preoccupied with getting ahead or around some obstacle, we can miss the peaceful support that is already within us. If we are distracted by the noise to produce, sell, and do better, then we are more likely to put less conscious effort in what we are doing. There is a practice of being attentive in work as there is with every other part of living. Work becomes a meditation, a central part to building a conscious life.

The love in the silence has specific plans for us. With our hearts open, the voice of the stillness inside us speaks clearly to trust this love, our true guide and employer. People who are tested in their work are being challenged in their belief in how present the silence is and how much it provides and cares for them.

The struggle for survival is moved by the fear that we are all alone and the world is against us. The love in the quiet reminds us that we live in God's midst, which is full of purpose and meaning and caring. It is through living in the monastery without walls that our worries about survival give way to trust in the silence. The sacred moments melt our fears, giving way to a practical life full of the joyous essence.

We are each called to a work that gives fulfillment. Fulfilling work separate from a life full of silence is not possible. We are called to work for the silence, in the silence, with the silence, and feel the love of the silence working through us.

SERVICE

Our concerns about work turn into our desire to serve. If we have found safety in the silence, we are less concerned about ourselves and more concerned about all other beings and the preservation of the earth. In the silence we are no longer just one soul in a world of souls needing souls. We are a soul representing the ocean of silence and wanting to help other souls feel the common ocean that is with us. As we move from concern about ourselves to concern about others, we move from absorption with ourselves to absorption with the silence. This encourages our openness and compassion. Service is the expression of the silence, love in action. It is not so much in the big things we do but in the little ways we receive others and care about them.

Many people wish to change their job to one that serves others. But in order to do so they must make the transition from working for themselves to working for the benefit of others. People rarely leave a well-paying job in sales or in a business office simply to find another well-paying job in social work or counseling, because the silence requires more from us in service. To give more to others we are called to give more of ourselves. As we honor the needs of others, we find new respect for ourselves. We give to others as they begin to find the silence working within them, guiding them, moving their lives so that they too can represent the love in the silence. Without our noticing, without knowing the vast efforts, without our appreciation, the quiet love is giving and giving through us and to us. The love in the silence is providing a constant example of service. This is why the path of service closely reflects the nature of the quiet realms, selfless in service. To serve is to merge with the silence and to give without needing applause or expecting anything in return. A soul who has opened to a life of service receives directly the gratitude and appreciation from the divine love.

Monks and mystics seek to follow the path of service, because to serve is to follow the footsteps that the silence is repeatedly placing before us. The silence is asking us to serve others so that the silence can serve us. Service is a pathway to the silent affection that can become our all, our motivation, and our gratification.

And what is service? Service is usually not in the large things we do, because these things are so often filled with our own need to be important and successful. Service is in the small things we do for one another to make the simple moments of life beautiful. Service can be taking a moment to light a candle at a meal. Service can be taking people we are thinking about a step further and including them in our prayers. Service is being available to someone we don't really consider a friend. Service is going out of the way for someone, giving more when we want to give less. We can do this as we become aware that we are giving to the silence in the other. And every gift to the silence is also a gift to ourselves and everyone. Service is being present, genuinely listening to a soul in trouble or great joy. Service is caring. Service is being quick with patience and slow to anger. Service is saying yes instead of following our fearful impulse to say no. Service is staying when we want to leave. Service is finding time when there is no time, deciding to listen when we feel a need to talk. And service is talking when it would be easier to say nothing at all. Service is doing the difficult things we would rather have someone else do. The path of service calls us, pulls and stretches us, and at times crumbles us to a greater path of service.

The path of service quickly leads us to resistance, selfishness, laziness, and hopelessness about giving something of real value. This list of obstacles to service can be seemingly endless. Our shortcomings can make us turn to the silence for help in going beyond ourselves to offer something that will last. We find we cannot really serve without calling upon the presence of the silence to be with us. Service can teach us to depend upon this peace for everything we do. On the path of service there are times we feel as though we are being used, and then there are times we are certain we are discovering our soul's true dimensions and the great divine care where no difficulty is too much, no need too great.

Great souls travel the path of service where courage is to be as small as we are yet represent the silence that is so vast. We begin the path of service again and again in this moment, being the most of who we can be, giving to the need before us. The silence is asking for our attention.

THE MONASTERY

Once we look beyond appearances, life in the monastery with walls is not so different from life in the monastery without walls. The monk or mystic inside us is challenged to live in touch with the presence of silence. We are called to discover in our relationships the sharing and quality of being that opens us and gives us more sacredness. Our sexuality can lead us to the most intimate experiences in the stillness, the devotion, in which we receive the quiet-filled affections. Whether with a partner, as part of a community committed to God, alone in nature, or in our own process of creativity, we find that sexual energy is literally the energy of creation. As we seek a life where our true needs become known, we recognize the difference between these needs and those that just keep us from feeling the love in the silence. With our growing awareness, it is natural for us to desire to work less for ourselves and more for others. Life is not separate from our pursuit of the sacred but is full of the opportunities for love and silence. The sacred is never very far away.

Life would be very busy without the presence of silence to slow us down and remind us of our purpose. We are reminded that we are living with the sacred silence all around us and within us. In all that comes to us in the vast quiet, we join the great tradition of monks and mystics not necessarily in what we do but in how much of ourselves we put into being and service. Every small gift goes a long way toward touching the presence of silence in those we give to. Life as service affirms the silence, protecting and honoring it for generations to come.

Everyday life is our stained glass window in the cathedral of the silence. In each relationship are the Mother and Child, the Father and Holy Spirit, our companions in the stillness. Our cloister garden has no walls and is found in everyone. And the more often it is found, the clearer we hear a voice in the simple peace calling us closer.

CHAPTER FIVE

PATHWAYS INTO THE SILENCE

Despite its omnipresence and promise of great love, the silence is often difficult to enter and stay in. Through the ages nuns and monks have discovered the sacred pathways on which to know the still oneness, the pathways that help us to become available to the many qualities of love. Some of these pathways are easy to find, while others are a real challenge. For every soul who searches there is at least one path that leads to the sacred silence. For within every soul is the knowledge to find the quiet presence that is full of the true purpose for each of us. Life must include these pathways, which are just right, genuinely practical yet holy.

RESPECT

Respect is something we give to someone whom we love, who in our eyes has worked hard, given much, or earned a special place in our hearts. We give our parents, friends, professionals, scientists, and famous people respect, for in our eyes they have achieved honor and esteem. In the eyes of the silence everyone deserves respect, for each soul's struggles and accomplishments are intimately known. Each being's essence is felt, appreciated, and held sacred in the Intimate Being or God. Respecting all living things is a specific pathway for going further into the silence and learning how the stillness holds a special place for each of us.

———————

Life in every culture reaches its finest moment in direct proportion to the degree of respect every member receives. Respect is called especially for those members who are rejected or cast aside. Inasmuch as we find time to spend with others and find value in them, we are very close to the awareness held in the silence. A culture that respects its members beholds the silent beauty in them in every season of life.

———————

We find ourselves respecting the small details of life like each other's feelings, as we become aware of the quiet in the little moments. Like the scientists who have recently confirmed how the small organisms in the ocean depths affect the entire food chain for the planet or how the rain forests in South America affect the quality of air everywhere, we come to respect the seemingly small things in life and understand their true importance.

Respect, the honor and esteem we hold for the circumstances of our lives, can reveal the intricacies, the subtle yet precise workings that are taking place in the great stillness. With respect, all of life fills us with purpose, the purpose that is held and honored in the silence. By developing respect for all beings, our feelings, and our path no matter what turns or bends appear before us, we awaken to how right and perfect our path is. We develop respect for others as we come to value ourselves. Our own being is valued as we practice feeling and enjoying the silence. Love gives us value. As we learn to find love in life's small moments, we learn to respect them as gifts of untold value. Respect teaches us to be less judgmental and more patient, less inclined to change ourselves and others and more appreciative of everything that life presents to us. No encounter, no experience, is unworthy of respect. Respect helps us to pick up everyone in our lives and hold them up to the light of the silence. Life in the sacred way is known differently from the everyday world by the amount of respect we bring to one another.

LISTENING

A respectful attitude means that we are ready to receive what comes to us. Respect is a way of listening for silence.

———————

The silence speaks as we listen . . .

———————

Taking the time to listen, we hear the quiet presence in each other. The silence speaks between our words. Respect gives us the patience to listen, the opportunity for qualities of stillness to fill us instead of the empty words we usually settle for. Listening helps us to become less impulsive with our wants and desires and more attentive to the needs of others. The practice of listening tunes our perception to the subtleties of each other's presence, in each voice, in every part of life. Listening takes us further into the silence. We can hear the words that are present even though they are not spoken. These words stay in the silence between us until someone is willing to receive them. Listening, we relieve the silence of the love it carries. The still presence in us listens, supporting the great presence of silence in everyone. If we listened to our interior being, we certainly would not live with so much noise in the world. We would settle for nothing less than the pure words, the words of substance.

Meanwhile, the true words that come from the silence within us, the sounds of the heart that are wrapped in perfect stillness, will naturally have our sincere respect as we hear them. Listening leads us into the sacred silence where we learn how much we are heard, whether we are speaking or not.

DEVOTION

The experience of listening to the silence can bring us to the experience of devotion. Active listening can create a very clear and pure path of devotion into the great quiet. Everyone seeks some object in their lives to which they can give complete devotion. Complete devotion is the opportunity to give ourselves fully with no reservations. Usually we hold ourselves back from devoting ourselves to others because we are afraid of their reaction. The silence can be the one place where we can unravel our heart's desire slowly in complete devotion. Where as partner or a job may be incapable of receiving all our love, the silence receives as much of ourselves as we are willing to give.

Devotion is giving our thoughts and feelings, love and fears, hopes and expectations, to the silence. By offering ourselves to the perfect stillness, the silence offers itself to us. By giving ourselves in devotion to the peace-filled quiet, the noiseless world gives us love's purity. Often we are afraid to give too much of ourselves to people because we feel they might become dependent upon our gifts. So we don't give all that we can. It is the silence where we can come again and again, giving our all. As we give more of ourselves to the silence, we learn the joy of giving to the silence often, in more parts of our lives. This path can be difficult in a culture that stresses independence and watching out for oneself. But people who overcome their fears and hesitation experience real devotion. The silence feels very close to them and full of tenderness.

———

Devotion flows when we are on our knees recognizing the throne of love inside the stillness. Devotion flowers when we are invited to care for the silence in someone in need.

———

Caring and humility are very close to the practice of devotion. With practice the purity of devotion seems to cover our troubles in a blanket of peace. Devotion is a quality very much in demand by love everywhere, the unrecognized yet very real love in the silence. In our meditations and prayers, pouring ourselves into the vast quiet in devotion is to experience a forgiving stream pouring back into us. To practice giving ourselves completely in devotion is to feel the great devotion given to us in the silence. Each small act of devotion, the little ways we care for one another, tie us inexplicably to the devotion of the silence toward all life. Devotion to life's small details increases the beauty of where we live and adds to the joy of those we live with. The little requests we respond to, the simple acts of love we give, mirror the devotion the presence in the stillness has for us.

SIMPLICITY

A practice of devotion is not possible in a complicated life. Devotion calls for simplicity in which we can feel the pure current of love with no interference from the world.

———————

Simplicity provides a very practical path deep into the silence. Simplicity carries the resolution to any question, feeling, and difficulty. Simple beginnings make for simple endings. Simple mornings make for simple afternoons and simple evenings. Simple gifts make for packages filled with love of the silence.

———————

Simplicity is a matter of the heart. Our minds can be busy thinking one thought after another. Our bodies can be busy doing one thing after another. Simplicity is the art of keeping a peaceful heart. The thoughts and actions that come from a peaceful heart stay within the silence. Life no matter how busy or quiet remains simple.

With simplicity life cannot become too complex or lost in activity. Simplicity keeps us very close to the stillness in everything we do. With simplicity our actions and our goals become aligned with those of the silence. Our thoughts and actions spring out of the peace of our inner world if peace is our priority. The simplicity keeps us free from the drive and need to be important. Our wholeness depends upon life being devoted to simplicity. Our hearts can become the fountain that pours the simplicity of the quiet back into us.

Simplicity is living in the present and feeling the present living in us. It is a risk to live in simplicity. If we lead a simple life, we have no need to blame others or circumstances for our problems. Simplicity is seeking refuge neither in future hopes nor in past blessings but in living simply now. Simplicity is feeling how much lightness is available in the moment to touch our shadow. Simplicity quickly gets us through life's challenges instead of making them complex and postponing them for another day. By going into our heart's peace first, the answers come more and more simply. If we practice living in the peace-filled presence, our living becomes more simple. This simplicity helps us find our way no matter what the difficulty.

As we desire the simple life, the silence comes closer to us. The simple life is measured not so much by what we do but by how much love we put into each thing we do. Simplicity opens a new world, a world of wonder, by showing us how much love can be found in the simple things like preparing a meal, walking in the garden, or delivering a gift to someone in need. Giving, receiving, gentleness, patience, and joy take on new meaning in a life of simplicity.

Simplicity is simply taking life's moments one at a time and appreciating them. With simplicity each meeting has more meaning. Simplicity is taking the time to value what is happening. Simplicity comes easier and more naturally as we respect, listen, and devote ourselves to the silence.

As simplicity helps us live in the present, more full of the quiet wholeness, those of us who are committed to a simple life feel the ground underneath and appreciate others around us.

FEELINGS

A life of true simplicity brings many feelings that we were too busy to feel before. The search for simplicity can bring feelings of emptiness, fear, anger, disappointment, hurt, and hope. With simplicity all our feelings are more present because there is nowhere to hide.

Each of us has feelings that occur naturally and spontaneously. Feelings express the silence within us. The silence can be experienced through joy, sadness, excitement, and all other feelings. Along with many ordinary feelings that pass hardly noticed, each of us also has doubts and fears that can seem overwhelming. Compulsive feelings, feelings of being out of control, are common for people who have not opened to and received the peacefulness of the silence. For example, some people have fears of poverty that keep returning. These fears may represent their separation from the quiet presence and inability to let go and fill themselves with their own wealth of silence. Recurring fears speak from the void where we have not received the peaceful silence. They come from the places inside that we have not surrendered to and allowed the presence of silence to care for. So we live with our fears and keep struggling instead.

Such feelings represent parts of our lives that have lost the wholeness of the silence. Our out-of-control feelings can be reactions to situations that are similar to those we experienced in childhood, when we were separated from the love in the silence through such traumas as birth, loved ones leaving us, and the like. The childhood experiences of separation carry emotional scars. Many people try to lead spiritual lives without having healed the emotional scars caused by the first denial or rejection of our solitude, our life in the silence. Moments of peaceful stillness will often remind us of the relationships and situations in which noise has taken over and the integrity of our own silence was denied.

We can stop being victims of childhood trauma, insensitive parents, an unloving church, the first encounters that invalidated us by developing a new awareness and relationship with the lingering feelings. These hurts continue to cause pain and call for the love in the stillness. The compulsive parts of our personality are usually about these feelings which are still hurting for affection, the affections of the silence. The out-of-control parts of our lives are filled with feelings waiting to be opened to, accepted, and given to the silence. The past remains heavy, a burden as long as it is carried separate from the silence. The past dissolves in the abundant love and support of the present. The future depends upon us opening to the infinite care possible in our relationship with the silence.

Feelings separated from the silence have led to the personality being separated from the soul. Feelings freed of their noise, naturally find a home in the silence where life and the soul are intimate with each other.

The people connected with our hurts are also suffering from separation of the silence. We discover compassion for those who hurt us by realizing that they too were suffering, that they too were unable to feel the affections of the peaceful quiet and hurt others instead. Having compassion for ourselves and the others involved in our pain is a necessary step in restoring the wholeness of silence. With compassion for ourselves and others we can begin to let our most difficult feelings guide us to a new and richer relationship with the silence. Everyone carries his or her own load of hurts. Healing these hurts can lead us to an entirely new life, a life in which we become responsible for living and preserving the sacredness of our own silence. When the hurt that has been passed on from generation to generation is healed, the patterns of pain are broken. Our therapy is to find the pathway into the silence that restores our being in sacredness. Whether through respect, listening, devotion, or simplicity, we heal our wounds fully as we recapture a sense of sacredness. The presence in the silence is what provides this element of love. Today's healing technology, theories and therapies are incomplete without our being conscious of the importance of silence and the role that silence has in healing.

The monastery without walls is the place where old hurts turn into wells of holy silence, where pain has been turned into soil for new flowers in the cloister garden. Sooner or later the unhealed noise in every feeling is restored in the pure life of the silence.

Sadness, joy, hurt, excitement, and every other feeling have a place in the silence. As we learn not to mask our feelings, deny them, or make them more important or less important than they are, we accept the challenge to bring our feelings to the quiet place inside where they can be completely received and healed.

Passing our feelings back and forth from one person to another, during an argument, for example, often overloads an already overloaded situation. Simply expressing our feelings or intellectually understanding them does not necessarily mean our feelings are valued and accepted. Sharing our feelings with someone who is ready to listen allows the silence in both of us to play its role as healer. In the meantime, we can learn to be with our feelings, accepting them as the presence of the stillness is accepting us. It is the silence that can truly hold what we feel without making anyone wrong or different. Our wholeness depends upon our learning to trust our feelings into the silence while inviting the silence to care for us.

Life's sacredness invites us to listen to each feeling and give it the respect and acceptance it deserves. Our feelings can open the unexplored pathway into our interior life, our life in the silence. Each feeling can lead to a new experience in the still places. The depths of our feelings lead us to new depths in being. The extent of our feelings can lead us to the extent we have not accepted parts of ourselves and others. We can never trust our feelings too much. Even anger and hate are not enemies to avoid. These feelings have power and energy that we have not been able to integrate and harmonize with our being. Anger and hate in particular need our attention so that we can receive their energy, make peace with them, and then find our heart again in the simple quiet.

In the silence is the understanding where each feeling finds it purpose. Each edge, nuance, and intensity of emotion has a place where it belongs and is received. Each feeling carries an opportunity for us to listen and to be led closer to where we really want to be in the heart of the stillness. Our feelings brought to the silence reveal how our entire being is accepted. In the vastness our feelings are simple energy, energy for the purposes of the silence. Following feelings as a pathway to oneness means returning 'home' with each feeling we embrace.

Boredom, anger, sadness, joy, each emotion when taken purely for itself leads us to a fresh knowledge of the silence. Boredom gives us a pause so that the quiet can rush in and refresh us with wonder again. Hurt is but a hidden pocket of energy, a disappointment that the still place within can receive and then care for. Sadness can be the simple calling to seek again the love in the silence for the attention we really want. And joy, perfect joy, is the spiritual union of the great quiet picking us and the whole universe up in its arms.

———

Each emotion denied or ignored is another lost opportunity for silence. Feelings repressed or circumvented limit the great love of the silence that is available to us. Each feeling has silence inside, waiting to be valued.

———

HAPPINESS

If there is one feeling that all other feelings lead to, if there is one feeling that becomes fuller and more alive when all other feelings are accepted, it is happiness.

Happiness, the pure joy of the heart, is not found accidentally or by luck. Happiness is not inherited or given once and for all, some people destined to have it and others not. Happiness, the heartfelt joy, must be received again and again. It is offered in the silence. Happiness is not determined by our life circumstances. It is shaped and formed out of the home we make for it in the still peacefulness, in our silent-filled life, in our monastery without walls. The silence's essential quality comes forth through happiness, ready to pour itself into everyone who holds space in his or her life to be happy. The silence loves the open heart, who is ready and poised for simple happiness. As we decide what will make us happy, the silence meanwhile is already here, ready to give, needing no reason to share the perfect joy. Happiness is virtually ever-present when a place of peace is kept inside just for happiness and nothing else.

DESIRE

Happiness leads us to a never-ending stream of desires. Feeling our desires and fulfilling them can keep life full and happy.

Some people believe that to live in a monastery with the sacred silence it is necessary to give up one's desires. This is not true. The test is to find our true desires. In fact the monk or mystic desires very much the peace and love in the silence, not compromises and unhappiness. The problem is not that we have too much desire. The problem is that we have too many desires. How much is our desire for more money, new possessions, fancy foods, vacations, and so on simply the thoughts we project onto our heart's hunger for the peace and quiet of the stillness? How many of our desires are just our mind's attempts to fulfill our soul's need for the purity and the fullness of silence? In all the little things we desire, our hunger for real love and joy gets lost. The more we try to make the things of this world satisfy us, the less desire there is for simple peace and quiet.

Let us feel our soul's hunger so intensely that the silence must bring us the pure answer. Let us desire so intensely that we will not confuse daily comforts and the love that is eternal. Let us desire so intensely that if necessary, every bone in our body will crumble and the silence will come and pick us up in sweetness and carry us away.

We can give each other the courage to feel the great desire with the collective recognition and importance we place upon living with the pure silence. Inside life's monastery, the stillness sits empty, waiting to be filled with our soul's attention. There is no gift of the silence that would be withheld from us. The simple life helps us realize the difference between the genuine peace and the material comforts that lessen our fears. But this does not mean that we cannot enjoy life's physical comforts and joys! Only that we do not limit our thirst and satisfactions to what we possess or hope to have. We allow ourselves to thirst more so that we can find the satisfactions that last, that come from the core of the silence.

Desire is not something to be ashamed of, ignore, or deny. It is through our desire that the silence knows how to love us. It is in the purity of our desire that the quiet can most purely be with us. Without our thirst how could the still presence so deeply fulfill us? The objects of our desires, the things we think we want, are provided for us, are available to us. But the silence loves the soul who has the courage to come directly for the love instead of settling for the substitutions. Desire is the lifeline of a spiritual path.

People living in a traditional monastery can too easily hide from everyday desires, deciding they are not worthy. But in the monastery without walls we can be preoccupied too easily with everyday desires, thinking they are necessary. What is our true desire, the thirst that waits behind our wants? Are we willing to feel our heart's wish? This is what the sacred silence asks from us.

NAKEDNESS

Most of us are unwilling to open to our deepest desire because we are afraid of the nakedness from which it comes. It is seemingly easier to live a life of noise and practical compromise than to seek the pure sound that only the pure heart, which is naked and humble, can know.

On the path of nakedness we wear our vulnerability, feeling the joys and sorrows, the hopes and disappointments to everyday life into the quiet place. As we take the time to accept our nakedness and give up the compulsion to cover ourselves, we feel the stillness covering us. As we take the time to feel our human vulnerability and give up our need to protect ourselves, we become more aware of the silence protecting us. The path of nakedness is a daily practice of accepting our simple nakedness. To be alive is to be sensitive and open and even afraid at times. When we are in touch with life's vulnerability, we are available for the wholeness and care of the silence.

No matter how many clothes we wear, how many possessions we have, how much knowledge we have, or how important we are in the eyes of others, we stand naked before the mirror of the silence. We come into the world naked and in the silence we leave the world naked.

The simple presence is the quiet witness to our entire life. Love's presence in the silence knows who we are even when we do not know ourselves. This love has already accepted every part of us that we have yet to accept; it loves every part of us we have yet to embrace. Life's events are either difficult or easy, depending upon how much of a commitment we have made to accepting our own nakedness.

The path of nakedness promises to take us further and further into the perfect oneness as we learn to depend upon the silence for every need and comfort. This is why the great nuns, monks, saints, and mystics had so few worldly desires and possessions. Their desire for sacred silence had become their first and last concern, and love's presence was everything to them.

After I have asked ten thousand times who will care for me, the silence answers very simply by providing the same care it has provided every other time I have asked . . .

COMMITMENT

So how do we protect our nakedness? In the ordinary world we can be compulsively busy with meetings and appointments, which adds to our sense of self-importance and helps us escape from the reality of our nakedness. But the monastery without walls offers the love of the silence, giving us less need to escape. We need nowhere to go. Our commitment to the silence is what helps hold the monastery together and the love of the silence near us. With commitment our nakedness is dressed in purpose. Each vulnerability, our fears and tenderness, is cared for if we are committed to bringing it to the source of care, the love that is in the perfect stillness.

We realize how committed the silence is to us and all of life as we stand steadfast in our own commitment.

The commitment to know the divine in the silence is not separate from any other commitments we make. When we make commitments to people, projects, and goals, we are committing ourselves to the silence in them. This is why we keep our commitments, because the silence in everyone and everything depends upon us. As part of the great harmony we find ourselves not wanting to be late for engagements and not needing excuses when we are. As the silence respects, we respect the words and behavior of others, knowing their words and behavior can come from their heart of silence. The quiet presence inside us asks us to make fewer and fewer commitments and put more love into everyone.

Life in the silence depends upon each soul honoring commitments. The strength of our everyday commitments strengthens our relationship with the silence. Our everyday commitments can be what holds the spiritual walls of our monastery in place. Our daily commitments can be our spiritual backbone, the cornerstone for our spiritual life.

Most of us choose not to join monasteries because we do not want to make such a commitment. Nevertheless, our lives demand just as great a commitment and just as much of our attention. If our relationships, work, and prayerful journey are to lead us to the sacred that is permanent and true, why would we withhold any part of us? Why would we withhold our commitment to a life of golden silence?

PEACE

Commitment comes easier as we enjoy the fruits that the pathways into the silence yield. From each pathway comes a peace, a peacefulness inside peace that assures us our commitment is not wasted and that brings us closer to the pure heart of stillness.

When people picture the peaceful life in the traditional monastery and then look at their own stressful life, the two seem irreconcilable. Our commitment to the peace in the silence is what can bring reconciliation between what we hope for and how our life is. The monastery with walls and the monastery without them may seem very far apart. When we can picture the peace inside the monastery, we are beginning to touch the peaceful part of us. When we can imagine the experience of living and praying in the cloister garden, we are beginning to move closer to our own interior garden. Commitment makes the difference between the occasional peace we feel and the sacred peace that transports us into the silence.

The monastery with or without walls has no guarantees of peacefulness. Many monks and nuns have found physical shelter in monasteries, but their souls were not prepared to deal with the silence. And many people living in the world have found themselves taken by such a holy peace that life's noise no longer has any hold over them.

There is a specific pathway of peace into the silence. This path does not wait for a change in world events and is not limited to the occasional crisis crying for peace. The path of peace is a daily effort to invite peace into every relationship and circumstance. Instead of struggling, we can invite peace as our struggles begin. Instead of projecting problems onto others, we can invite peace in the silence to give us back our wholeness. Instead of resisting and worrying, or going out of our way to salvage a bad situation, we can invite peace to be with us right now. This peace can help us embrace any situation, every feeling.

Peace is the feeling that knows no obstacles. Peace is the experience that strengthens our being yet confronts our lives in so many ways. Peace is the original state of the great quiet. When we learn how immense the peace is, it flows in like a stream of light. Peace can seemingly come crashing down upon our lives if we do not know how to receive it. Peace can knock over our lives and all the walls we erect to protect ourselves from it. Peace can be very gentle, like waves lapping at the shore. But the power of peace can be frightening, at least in the beginning, for those who become aware how separate their lives have been from the presence in the silence. True peace can open questions about everything in our lives that is not peaceful.

———————

With peace as our desire, sooner or later we may have no choice but to make peace with everyone and every part of our life. This is the peace that builds the simple life that is pure and true. This leads us to the lightness of peace, which is so much a part of sacred silence. Simply inviting peace into our relationships, work, and home can have a profound effect on us. Making a commitment to have peace in our lives is a sincere act of courage requiring genuine humility. In our determination to make peace, we are supported by the oceans of peace that exist in the vast stillness.

———————

The monastery without walls asks us to practice peace instead of complaining about the lack of it. The path toward the peace of the silence is very direct. We must be on the lookout for the approaching moments. Then, as peace approaches we can surrender, and let it pass through us. We are called to give up our self-importance and feel the peace holding us. And if we are afraid of disappearing in the endless body of peace, we can face our own insignificance directly and feel the peace helping us. Peace can be very sweet and personal for a soul who tries to live a life full of the presence of peace.

———————

Following the path of peace into the stillness, we may find ourselves eating less, sleeping less, being less busy. With peace we find ourselves wanting less because the peace seems to give so much. With peace we are brought face to face with the love that knows no limits.

LOVE

Love and peace are flowers that grow out of the same soil. Love includes a beautiful peacefulness and peace opens us to love. The love that includes peace tells us that we have found the love that lasts forever, the love that is sacred.

So often we long for love and complain that there seems to be so little. So much of life is built around the need for love but so little attention is given to the primary source of love in the silence. Love is so important and yet we know so little about how to open love's true doors. Instead we place our expectations for love on a partner or a project. And it is no wonder that we are eventually disappointed. For who or what could represent the love in the silence other than the purity of the silence itself? At best our partners and projects can give us the love and support to seek the great love, the Intimate Being that is revealed to us in our relationship with the pure stillness.

There is only one love great enough, large enough, and worthy enough for us to spend our entire lives dreaming of, to chase after, and to make fools of ourselves over, to risk everything for, to invest every effort and all hope in, and to fully open to, and this is the divine love in the silence.

Holy people, past and present, are recognized by the inordinate amount of love they can possess. Their faces are filled with love's presence as they live and work with all walks of life. They have learned love's greatest lesson, which is not to limit love to one source. Their lives are examples of being open to love in all the small and grand ways it comes. This is the central mystery of the monastery without walls; ordinary life can be a treasure of love's presence. As we pursue pure love, we see that life is full of love's opportunities. Some of the most ordinary parts of life, for example, spending time with a salesperson who comes to our door, taking an evening walk through our neighborhood, or watching the wind blowing through the trees, can open us to love's greatest presence. It is the monk or mystic inside us who dissolves our limits and discovers love's many moments.

Life in a monastery can be as limiting as life in any other location unless the monks and nuns are always willing to find a new relationship with the love in the peaceful quiet. The apparent shortage of love results from our inability to appreciate all the love that is with us. Love joins us in our awareness of the present. There are so many gifts of the moment needing only our awareness. The pathway of being alert to love's presence opens the common moments to the divine, the ordinary moments to love's power of transcendence. In our willingness to be open and naked to love, love's silence creeps up inside us.

———

Love crumbles strength that is not true, holds up what is small and beautiful, and praises itself everywhere in everyone.

Love in its purity unveils a soul until all the fear is exposed. Then love wraps us in a blanket of snowlike softness.

Love in its simplicity shows us that our busyness is leading us nowhere, because there is nowhere to be but with love. Then love in its holiness gives us everything we always wanted, simply, directly from the silence.

———

We are called to recognize the difference between sacred love and the sentimental attachments we seek security with; love that affirms wholeness and love that attaches itself to make oneself okay. There is the love that makes our higher self be compassionate, honest, and giving. And there are the emotional needs we call love that excite us about love's possibilities yet keep us dependent and unhappy. While we search for, struggle with, and gain and lose faith in our romantic relationships, the great love is always with us, begging us to receive it.

We can feel our desire to collect all the faith invested in the wrong places through the years and seek to bring it back to the feet of love, the silence. The silent life receives everything we offer, every desire, every feeling, every wish without ever turning away. In the heart of silence, there is the one love that is true enough to depend upon; the great quietude within us. This is the love that takes us beyond whatever we imagined love to be.

As we give ourselves to this love we find it asking us how much we are willing to receive. This is the question challenging us again and again throughout every season of our life. As life in the world is convinced that daily struggle is a part of it, life in the monastery without walls is confronted with our self-imposed limits to receive all that is being given. A soul devoted to the silence risks everything for this love that unifies us with our true spiritual home.

GRATITUDE

Those who know the divine love, the root of the soul, find a well of gratitude within. Gratitude is a distinct part of the love in the silence. The many thank-you's said each day add to the sweetness of the little moments, as if the blossoms in the monastery grow more fragrant. Our spiritual practice is the brick and mortar of the monastery without walls. And our interior walls become an invisible fortress when built out of gratitude and love. The path of gratitude strengthens the presence of silence in us and in the world.

It is said that a soul who never meditates, never prays, and doesn't even believe in the infinite silence as the home of God, will still reap the benefits of the great presence if he or she leads a sincere life full of gratitude.

Gratitude from the bottom of the heart touches every corner of the vast stillness. Gratitude for the little blessings each day builds a pile of blessings in the silence as well as physically in front of us. Gratitude leads us to appreciate the little gifts that life brings. The small joys become noticeable even in the midst of difficulties. The path of gratitude can help us keep in touch with the gifts of life. As we develop awareness from living in the moment and appreciating what comes from such moments, gratitude will naturally grow in our heart. During good times, the grateful experience only deepens. And in hard times, a heart grateful for any blessing keeps us ready for better times.

The path of gratitude into the silence includes thankfulness for our defeats, mistakes, and pain in discovering new insights, renewed friendships, and life-giving changes we are prompted to make. Gratitude can also include thankfulness for our trials, inconsistencies, and hopelessness as we are led to explore life more deeply. Our challenges take us beyond our normal limits where we discover that our life is not "ours" but is inexplicably woven into a greater will, love's will, the will of the unvoiced wonder. In the silence reasons for gratitude always exist. We can be thankful for an illness because it brought us back to the path we had strayed from. We can be thankful for difficult times with a partner because we can perceive our own harshness, darknesses, and walls we erect to keep out love. We can be thankful for any crisis because we can move closer to the divine heart in the quiet as we ask for help. Being thankful for our life's path can keep us in the calm of the silence wherever we go. As we follow the path of gratitude, we discover our whole being, because no experience is shunned or avoided. Every day is included on the path of gratitude.

Gratitude is more than simply accepting life, it is actively practicing being thankful, which means taking the time to feel and appreciate our life. Being grateful can bring healing to illness, prosperity to poverty, happiness to sorrow. We can find gratitude during difficult times by developing the habit of looking for something to be grateful for. Right away our search begins loosening the attachments our difficulties have made to us. A life of gratitude teaches that we are not alone and that our life is part of the love of the beautiful oneness. Gratitude, the simple feeling of appreciation, restores a peace inside that brings more and more reasons for gratitude.

THE MONASTERY

Every monastery is a sacred space for exploring and experiencing the silence. Respect, listening, devotion, simplicity, nakedness . . . all these paths introduce the simple presence that love brings. The monastery without walls is free of tradition and perhaps more open to new ways into the silence. Meanwhile, the traditional monastery reminds us that no course is completed until we take it to the end. Without our silent commitment, it is too easy to think we have found a new path full of potential when we may be merely avoiding the rocks and bends on the path we are on. It is so easy to be distracted if we do not find our own spiritual discipline to live from.

Our sacred self lives with little support. Our search for silence, our prayer, and our meditation lead us and provide us with the way. It is the daily practice of taking our feelings into the quietude, remembering our nakedness, and being committed that gives us the support we need. This practice literally keeps us in touch with the silence. We can be held on our way by the quiet desperation we feel for a life that is sacred. As we commit ourselves entirely, the companion that stays with us no matter where we go is our companion in the silence. The monastery without walls is where all the different pathways lead to the sacred heart of love's silence. Here life has no walls except those we maintain until we are ready to become aware of the overwhelming peace and love.

CHAPTER SIX

MONASTERY WITHOUT WALLS

Where we encounter silence we rub up against our innermost self and find God touching us . . .

What exactly attracts us to life in a monastery? What is it that speaks to so many people over and beyond their feelings about organized religion? Surely it is more than the wish to be free from life's normal frustrations. After all, people can take vacations to relieve daily tensions. Does the monastery attract us because it offers an escape from life's burdens and routines? There must be easier ways to get away from the stress of modern living. Is the intrigue of a monastery just sentimental emotions? Or is the cry for the sacredness of a monastery our soul's way of expressing an unmet need for love, the need for spiritual love that only the depths of prayer and meditation can give? What makes the monastery so special? Certainly the regimentation, the social and sexual isolation, and the loss of personal identity a monk or nun endures are not what attracts most people. It is because of these things that most people turn their heads and begin looking for something else. Some people, however, have an overwhelming desire to run into God's arms yet have no place to go. There is a calling that stays with them. Practically speaking, they know they cannot lead the life of a nun or monk, but their heart is still open, seeking sacred experience. What is it that suggests to us that we are part monk or nun? What is it that tells us that we are both ordinary and mystic with a life to lead in the monastery without walls?

THE CLOISTER GARDEN

In the center of many traditional monasteries is the cloister garden. In the West, Christian monasteries typically have a peace-filled courtyard with planted or potted flowers around a brick well, surrounded by ancient walls. In the East, many Buddhist monasteries have the rock and gravel meditation garden, the Ryoan-ji. In their cloister garden, monks and nuns have wandered, meditated, prayed, and reflected, letting the quiet perfection of the flowers in all their seasons proclaim the perfection of life. The peace in these gardens can be compared to heaven, or rather heaven can be compared to the cloister garden. For some people the cloister garden is perhaps the only place that fully speaks to them, the place where heaven and earth are indistinguishable. Here, nature and simple quiet and reverence have been held sacred, honored, and appreciated through the centuries. It is believed that angels protect this garden and that everything holy in the silence nurtures it. It is the cloister garden that holds the silence for the busy nun or monk to come back to again and again. It is as if the solitude found in this garden contains the feelings of God. Anyone willing to stop and feel the peace-filled presence can experience an overflowing of tears that are not only their own but God's as well.

———

In the silence of the cloister garden a human being is more than human, taking on the subtle wings of light. Nature is more than nature, flowing with the essence of life. People and plants take on the quality of the illumination, as they really are. Inside the sweet harmony of the cloister garden live all beings, those who have lived before and all beings unborn. Inside the holy stillness is the collective being; the wisdom, joy, and love freed and saved from the hearts of all. And all of this is just a small part of the immense being of God in the cloister garden.

Every prayer, every meditation that participates in the cloister garden participates in all such gardens through history and the desire for a life that is wholly sacred and blessed.

Each morning in the cloister garden is a new day begun in the bright light of the silence. And each evening among the still flowers is to end another day in the arms of the silence.

———————

Our soul, the mystic quality inside us, depends upon the cloister garden to be at the center of our lives. This is a place of refuge where we can develop our awareness of life's wonder. The cloister garden is a place of pure stillness where the quiet wholeness inside us can encounter itself, be, and find rest. In this garden the love in the silence everywhere finds its home. All beings who create a cloister garden in their heart add to the peace inside them, and give the silence another refuge, another place that is safe and protected. Such refuges are rare in these noisy days full of hardened beliefs and passions that are afraid of commitment and the discipline to know the fruits in the unspoken world.

The monastery without walls depends upon the peace from such a garden. We may not have the ancient stones or a well surrounded by flowers to remind us, but the monk or mystic inside us needs a sheltered spot, our own cloistered place that is held sacred and cared for. Perhaps more than ordinary monks and nuns, we need one place that is well defined, respected, nurtured, and held pure. In order for there to be perfect stillness in the heart, something in our lives must reflect the peace and beauty we live for. Every monk or nun needs some spot where the tender qualities of silence can be expected to prevail. We need a place where the beginnings of our awareness of silence can be planted, watered, and tended to maturity with prayer. Before the spirit-filled life can climb the spiral staircase into higher realms, we need a place to take root.

Our spiritual practice calls us every day to spend time in our own cloister garden in the heart, which gives meaning to everything we do. For sacredness to be more than a romantic notion, we must become conscious of our relationship with the earth, with the heaven in us and everyone about us. The simple presence everywhere is served by our creating a place where the sacred can make a home.

THE ALTAR

All places of worship have an altar where the silence holds the sacred for those who come to it. For Christians at the altar ordinary bread and wine are changed into the body and blood of Jesus Christ. In Buddhism, the pagoda provides the physical and symbolic point of orientation for everything seen and unseen. At the Hindu altar, rice, fruit, and nuts, and other ordinary foods become a holy sacrament. At every altar, words spoken with our full participation become prayers. Through our sincerity simple actions become rituals full of meaning, glimpses into the workings of the divine. Many people are critical of modern religion because it has limited the altar to a stone place inside large brick buildings, ignoring the other places in our life that are also holy. Some people believe the failure to include more silence, more love around the altar, has created a critically unbalanced world. They feel the need of the divine feminine image of God, nature, priests who are women, married couples, family, children, other rituals, dance, and sacred music in and around the altar to bring the wholeness the world is crying for.

But perhaps the problem is not only the style of worship and approach to the sacred but also the lack of worship, a lack of altars. We are responsible for limiting access to God to forms that feel dry or empty. As silence is in short supply so is the altar, the place where we develop a relationship with life's sacredness. Most religions today have limited participation for worshipers. People do not know how to focus their energy and develop their awareness to open to the blessings at the altar. Many people turn from the religion of their parents because it lacks movement, the five senses are not involved, and their souls are not touched. The monastery without walls includes many souls who have no specific spiritual home yet who have an intense spiritual desire to feel the presence of an altar in their lives. As we embrace beings of all religions or no religion, we should also embrace each other to find the forgiveness and compassion for the faults we found around the altars of our childhood. Today we have a new awareness that can help us go back and find the truth that was superceded by the unhealed noise in the church of our early years.

Meanwhile, whether our altar is in church, a vase of flowers and a candle in one room of our home, a special spot in nature we pass on the way to work, or a sacred place far away yet we know is there, altars keep the silent presence real for us. Through our altar, we become familiar with the quiet presence and can more easily carry it inside us. Whether with walls or without, every monastery needs an altar.

Creating a personal altar at home can become an ongoing source of spiritual expression and experience. Our personal altars are where we can put meaningful pictures and statues. They are where we can develop our relationship with the silence. Each altar has a different feeling depending upon what we bring to it physically and spiritually. Here the physical world becomes something more, an invitation for spirit. An altar invites the perfect presence to influence our lives. Simply maintaining an altar helps us to keep an awareness of the silence in other parts of the day as well. Having established the peacelike cloister garden in one part of our life, our personal altar, we can become sensitive to the silent altar about us and inside us. Our relationship with the altar grows as we practice bringing more of ourselves and our lives to this place.

The absence of silence leads to a form of pollution. The space that should serve the sacred is being filled with other activities and is spoiled, ruined slowly. Once the space is gone it is difficult to get back. The disappearance of the sacred from our lives cannot be measured, but the gradual reclaiming of the quiet can quickly be felt in the quality of our lives.

The reemergence of the silence in the world may depend upon the reappearance of altars in people's ordinary lives, in living rooms, rooms for healing and re-creation. As we rediscover the importance of silence we will want to build altars that offer the unsounded presence a home.

The traditional church holds a place for the heart to be taken hold of. Imagine our homes and other parts of our lives having a place reserved for the love in the silence. This would transform the monastery into a sanctuary that is less isolated and more available to the world. As everyday life flows from one activity in one room to another, life can flow from one altar to another, from one moment of peace and beauty to the next.

In some cultures people build altars everywhere. The Balinese in Indonesia, for example, build them in front of banks, in isolated fields, next to rivers, and at the front door of hotel rooms in the morning. They leave a flower and a few leaves to remind everyone that God is present. Despite the pressures of modernization, Bali remains an island afloat in another world, a world alive with the presence of silence. People in all parts of the world are struggling to maintain the sacredness in their traditions that are threatened by modern life. It is for each of us to reclaim, enliven, and focus our energies at the altar that expresses our inner life.

THE INTERIOR LIFE

At every altar the silence holds the space where it is safe to open to our interior life. An altar is made of love and devotion. This love and devotion is a softness welcoming our inner being, all that we bring to the altar. The oneness present is not neutral or empty but filled with the love and devotion we put into the altar. At the altar we have the opportunity to encounter the love and devotion at every altar, because human love and divine love are not separated by time or space. Each altar is a window into God's presence. The care and respect we put into the altar give reality to this window out of ordinary reality into the dimensions of stillness. Here each moment of self is received and held in its purity. Our fears and feelings of separation have no other place where they can be received and accepted as they are transformed into peace. Every time we bring a part of ourselves to the altar, our emotions and doubts are realigned with the presence of the altar and the sacred life inside us is reaffirmed.

Our interior life is made out of the same seasons that touch every creature. Winter's night, spring's rebirth, summer's joy, and autumn's surrender are part of our own interior seasons. The seasons of our interior life invite our investigation and appreciation. As we accept that we have seasons like nature, our interior life can blossom and bloom, wither and lie dormant, before being born again. In addition to the seasons, the elements of fire, water, earth, and air move everything in us as they move everything in nature. Each of us has had experiences with building and watching fires or sitting next to lakes or near the ocean. We have had special moments in nature while feeling the green earth or the air while viewing the expansive sky. Our connections to the elements are our connections to life's altar and the presence that nurtures and sustains us. Having our own cloister garden and altar brings a new sense of the elements alive in our being. We can see the perfection of our own seasons and rhythms. The cloister garden is the part of life that does not mold us but invites our soul's sensitivities. The altar includes the presence of silence that does not push or pull us in some direction but calls us to be present for what is sacred.

The garden has the water where everything is washed and made innocent. The great stillness here holds the great fire, where all that is not true is burned into ash. The garden is the earth, the home that welcomes all beings. The simple air we breathe becomes the source of all the faith that sustains us. As the invisible ether or the mysterious golden metal, the cloister garden holds everything together.

A full interior life gives our life in the world roots. We do not lose ourselves. Everyday noise and distractions pass us by because we are grounded in our own silent being. With the altar at the center of our interior life, our senses are doorways to the divine and life in the world is divine in action.

THE MONASTERY

Our cloister garden or altar is the center of the monastery without walls. As our images of divinity change, perhaps from pictures to just the stillness of one candle and one flower, we also change. Through the altar we offer shape and form to the silence inside us. Through the sweet presence within us, we find new realization and appreciation of our interior life. Our altar and cloister garden are the heart of our lives, the place that prevails over the noise we live with.

We have much to learn from our traditional brothers and sisters in monasteries about creating a sacred space that opens the way for sacred silence and sacred lives. Devotion that could appear as dull repetition, every morning and evening at the altar, resembles bees returning with more honey to the silence. Ordinary people become monks or mystics not solely through a discipline of prayer five times a day but through discovering their desire to pray many times a day. Keeping and maintaining an intimate space, an altar, helps keep the desire for silence alive and the relationship with the invisible visibly in front of us.

We become free of the fear that resides in the noise of everyday life when the cloister garden has grown around us. Life discovered in the garden's silence frees us from the tensions and traps of modern living. As our interior life becomes visible to us, we become more invisible to others. We are less in the world and more in the silence. We do not need to take up so much space. We do not need so much of everything. The cloister garden prevails inside us, giving us more perfect peace than we had ever imagined. As we find more riches in the beauty of the stillness, we develop our desire for beauty everywhere and to be available for love's silent touches. We bring more light into the world through the windows of our altar. Our lives become an extension of the cloister garden, which blossoms in more meaning.

Living in the monastery without walls we want to make as much room as possible for our interior life, for it is here that we experience the nuances and changing horizons of the love in the silence. We seek the work, play, and spiritual community that are simple and true so that we can be in touch with our interior experience. The monastery gives value to our feelings, daily experience, and beingness no matter how much we accomplish, or how we are recognized by others. This place of inner affirmation is what calls so many of us.

Once the richness of the sacred is rediscovered, ordinary riches offer so much less appeal. Our inner garden, the altar's light, is what is important. With our interior life the altar provides the pathways that make life in the world holy once again. The peaceful presence in the garden gives us the support to open to life's joy and to risk feeling the seemingly vast void we find inside us that often precedes new depths of joyful being.

The monastery without walls calls us to the garden, the place where our loving attention leads to the sacred fullness. This is the place inside us that brings wholeness to our conflicting feelings, soothing the tension between our interior life and the world we live in.

CHAPTER SEVEN

THE HUMAN ASPECTS

A commonly held view of life in a monastery is that of a protected, almost idyllic scene in which monks or nuns live simply and comfortably according to an old tradition of spiritual and social support. The monastic structure is thought to take care of one's needs for guidance and economic survival. We imagine grace-filled monks and nuns preoccupied only with daily prayer and meditation. But in fact, there is no special walk of life that has taken care of the physical needs of food and shelter in order to meditate and pray all day. No matter how strong their community, monks and nuns must interface with each other, work to support the community, and confront their inner struggles. The monastery with or without walls has no special means of physical support. Life cannot be protected from itself. The monk or nun in everyone faces life's vulnerability to change, making a living and building positive relationships. Those who participate in the sacred silence maybe can live without prestige, wealth, and social popularity, but the inner insecurities, the interplay between our doubts and faith, are still present. With a simple life we can live in relative obscurity, but the fears over our physical well-being can remain. What makes life different is how we receive the challenges before us while creating no need to find challenges that are not really there. After we have truly perceived life's difficulties we can begin the solution.

SURVIVAL

Daily survival is not only about having food to eat and shelter over our heads, but is also about looking at what is moving us to survive. Dreams, hopes, fantasies, and desires for too many people are broken or compromised by the pressures of life. Life for too many is lived from one need to another, from one paycheck to the next. The monastery without walls guides people back to a life where dreams and hopes come from, where life is a steady stream of spirit through which life becomes a continuous act of cocreation, our will and a greater will working together. As people turn from the noise of the world, the heart from which dreams originate begins to feel itself, recover, and thrive again. As we turn to the quiet presence, the love that makes dreams possible is felt to be within us. Survival is more than merely meeting basic needs; it is how much love is a part of our day, how much love we are bringing into the world. Contrary to the common perception that the monk or nun inside us must give up dreams to survive peacefully in the silence, we are called to give up the fear that suppresses our dreams so that we can be fully alive in the vast wonder. We are called to receive as much love as we can, then find our way of giving this presence to the world. In our closeness to the silence, we feel and know that the income and means to do what gives the most love is not only possible but is natural, supported by all the love in the stillness.

———

For life to become free of fear is to come to depend upon the silence as our father, mother, employer, best friend, companion, the divine cup from which we drink.

FEAR

Every day there are decisions we make, and words we say that are motivated either by our fear or by love. Alone in the noise-filled world we emotionally contract and act fearfully. Feeling the peaceful silence, we make decisions and choose words that are filled with the presence of faith. Our relationship to the silence very much determines how much we open to each other and life's opportunities or close and withdraw because of our fear.

What we usually spend time worrying about and what we are really afraid of are often two different things. In ordinary life we can worry about paying last month's bills and then struggle with next month's, thinking this is normal. We can worry and worry without ever looking at and silencing our true fear, which is alongside our vulnerability. Our fears can live on disguised in one worry and then in another until they are finally brought to the love in the simple quiet.

Most of us avoid the stillness because we are afraid. But we must remember that the quiet itself is not frightening, it is what we bring to the silence that disturbs us. The dismantling of the structures we build to avoid the silence is what is frightening. The silence exposes the relationships, work, and daily habits that are driven by our fears. The shelter we seek separately from the quiet, the companionship we search for away from the still-ness, and the eating and drinking habits that we may depend upon outside the silence are all created from our fear. The silence slowly sheds light on the parts of our lives that exclude the peace of the perfect presence. It is the thought of letting go of these structures and habits to find our place in the silence that is often frightening.

Fear can be an indication that we are letting go of false comforts to find the true comfort in the silence. Fear can be a sign that we are becoming aware of our unnecessary busyness, the loneliness we feel, the needs we usually ignore, including our need for peace and quiet. Fear emerges as our substitutes for the love in the silence no longer work, and only silence is present.

Through our fears, we can gain new insights into the still presence. If we are sensitive to the rivers of fear within us, we can learn to flow with them into the silence instead of running away from them. Life is full of such rivers.

———————

People shouldn't jump too quickly into long periods of naked silence, because life's daily structures they have built in place of the quiet presence can become shaky and threatened. In the stillness, the noise we live with can be felt inside. The thoughts and feelings that normally distract us from the silence can surface as our fear. In the gentle comfort of the oneness the parts of ourselves we are uncomfortable with become visible. The silence is like an intense bright light that shines on our uncertainty. It is like a clear mirror that reflects the doubts and fears we carry around with us.

The soundless presence has a special invitation for each one of our fears. Wherever we encounter ourselves and the silence, we cannot expel our fears. No great confrontation with our fears will result in their disappearance. The end to our fears is the acceptance of the sweet love of the silence. As we accept the simple quiet, simply and lovingly, we embrace our fears until we feel the sacred healing them. It is the sacred that changes our self-image and that accepted the fear in the first place. It is the sacred that transforms fear with the special love that does not include space for fear. In the meantime, until life is enhanced in the silence, restored with an identity including the sacred, one fear will often be replaced with another. One worry is solved only to be followed by another. Fear can persist in virtually every soul, every walk of life. No special teaching or partner, no health program or economic prosperity, can promise to eliminate it. Fear can live quite safely most anywhere, including in the strongest, bravest souls who use their strength or bravery to hide their fear. Other than the presence of love and understanding there are no special techniques to stamp out the fears of the darkness. Fears stay until we accept the love that is here for them, until we accept living in the unknown with the lightness of being, which comes from being conscious of the sacredness in the silence.

Fear continues because it is part of being human. But as we introduce fear to the safety of the silence we become stronger. Every fear filled with the peace of the stillness frees more of our wholeness. Our fears can signal our need for the gentle touch of the silence. Our fears can alert us to our core feelings of fear, which surround our need for the sacred love found in the lucid stillness.

LONELINESS

Fear represents our separation from the silence. We often experience this as loneliness. Because we are afraid of our dependency upon the quiet presence, we stand apart. The feeling of separation is so real that fear takes over. We compensate by working harder, eating or sleeping more, being surrounded by family and friends, wishing for future events or reminiscing about the past. We cover our separation from the great stillness and our loneliness in many ways. Instead of letting life take us away from our feelings, we can let our feelings invite us to come closer to the presence of love. Life's seasons, when family and partnerships grow apart and we are lonely, are the times when the silence wants us all to itself again.

During these times we usually do not know just how sacred such moments are for being alone and vulnerable for the love that is with us. We do not know how to respond and often turn to old relationships, standby projects, diet and exercise, or other activities to help us get through the difficult times. The difficult times, however, do not necessarily have to be the bad times we make them out to be. These are the moments that our souls are particularly naked and the silence is quite close. Our periods of loneliness can lead us to our unique relationship with the vast wonder as we find our way to feel the love.

Loneliness may be the strongest root holding our modern problems in place. Addictions, unhappy relationships and the compulsion for possessions may grow from this root. This root cannot be chopped off, because so much of what has been held up may fall down with it. This root cannot be pulled up, because what other roots would take its place and hold us up? Each of us in our own time is called to our innermost self and feels who we are to discover, how intensely the silence is present, how much we are loved. It is the wordless love entering our roots that holds us to the earth.

Loneliness can be perceived as a cry that the love in the silence gives us. Although difficult to understand, our times of loneliness can be the calls for renewed intimacy with the silence. Subtle whispers, gentle moments, and the blowing leaves carry the intimate conversation we have with the pure quiet. Being with the silence in these times is the key to feeling the love that is with us. Knowing our loneliness has a special purpose for us to meet in new depths of the stillness can help give us the courage to be available and not hurry for the lonely seasons to pass. In our prayers and silent vigils, we can cooperate with the noiseless order. A new relationship is evolving when times of loneliness are times for being alone, simply being by ourselves with the love in the silence.

EMPTINESS

Underneath the loneliness may be the fear of emptiness, of not having found security in the vast awareness. As the world pulls us away from experiencing ourselves in the silence, we are left with feelings of emptiness. We generally avoid these feelings because we do not know how to be with them and are unsure where they will lead us. To be simply empty, available for the mysteries in the silence, is to be present with our sacred self. What could be emptiness for silence is filled with all the things we are attached to. Whatever we do, whatever we plan, whatever we miss, our thoughts are full of ways to be anything other than empty for the presence in the simple quiet. Our life-style, relationships, diet, and identity are full of things we hold onto, leaving us with less room for the silence. The goal is not to have a vacant life with no attachments but to live each day, each moment, with more awareness, which yields greater openness and flexibility. To live life less determined to have our way, opens us to the ways of the silence.

To be empty is to practice letting go of the fears that possess us and to be more attached to the substance of life, the love in the silence. To be empty is to be available for the riches of the hidden harmony instead of the substitutions our fears would have us settle for. With emptiness as a friend we are brought to a new fullness of quiet, a fullness that has not settled for life's distractions, a fullness that comes from our commitment to a life in the silence. We make more room for emptiness as we value the wonder, the grand heights, and quiet recesses of silence. We find more emptiness as we commit ourselves to the mysteries worth beholding, to the inner life that has more space and appreciation to expand in our emptiness.

We can be aware that difficulties are an avoidance of emptiness. Difficulties occupy a space that could be available for the silence. The larger the difficulty the more space we have to find inside for the silence. What preoccupies us, what overwhelms us, what challenges us, is what we hold onto instead of a deepening relationship with the silence.

Through emptiness life calls us to listen to what occupies our attention. With the desire for emptiness guiding us, the food we eat, the work we do, and the rest we take can nourish and support our wish for emptiness, for the presence of silence. Emptiness is a state in which our desire grows for the love in the stillness. When the purpose of life is to find more space for the silence, we are doing all that we need to be doing. We simply want to remember that emptiness keeps us present, aware, and conscious of our place inside the unvoiced world of stillness.

_____

Emptiness keeps a place for the qualities of heaven to possess us. The golden bird is always in search of an empty nest in which to rest.

_____

SELF-IMPORTANCE

How we accept or resist opportunities for emptiness has a lot to say about the self-importance we hold onto. Self-importance tries to protect us from emptiness and the infinite terrain of the silence. Without self-importance we imagine we would be overwhelmed and would probably fall apart on our small island surrounded by the vast space of the stillness. But in truth our fear of the endless quiet keeps us pursuing recognition and honors, which offer little satisfaction compared to the great peace promised by the cloister garden, the monastery without walls. Self-importance resides in the things we do separately from the quiet presence to make us more secure, loved, noticed, important in our eyes or in those of others. Self-importance is what we try to give ourselves or others out of fear we will not find the love that waits for us in the silence.

We cannot get rid of self-importance recklessly by sudden life-style changes or by rigorous meditation or yoga. The roots of self-importance can take hold in any act of self-denial. The best way to be free of self-absorption is to ask the help of the silence. Toward the stillness we can direct our prayers for simplicity and humility. With the silence we can strive to make our lives ever more pure and true. We cannot free ourselves of self-importance with only our own efforts. Slowly, gently, with the help and grace of the noiseless world, we can get a glimpse of our true self in the golden love that awaits the silent heart.

Self-importance can hide its face in any activity we do. Whether we lead public or private lives, whether we are known by many or few, self-importance is the part of our identity that is based on fear. It is not what we do that determines our self-importance but how much fear is present as we are doing it. One clear way through our false identity, our self-importance, is the gift of service. Loving the hurt in others reminds us of our own vulnerability. Another clear way is simply to feel how our life can change at any time, remembering that in the end all that we can count on is the love in the stillness. Any truthful way of being enlivens us and lessens our false identity, and our need for self-importance.

PRIDE AND ARROGANCE

Self-importance is another term for pride or arrogance. Every life lived separately from the love in the silence may be a life blinded by arrogance. Our strengths, problems, work, relationships, and even our constant attention to our own growth can be forms of arrogance if they keep us separate from feeling our interior life and the unending quiet. Our minds can invent a false identity instead accepting our humble relationship with the simple presence. Pride takes form in so many ways. Even humility can be a form of pride if we enjoy the self-importance derived from acting humble. And what is so wrong with pride? Perhaps nothing, perhaps everything, because pride keeps us away from the experience of emptiness where the presence in the silence can be our all and everything. Pride is important to erase because of all its subtlety and pervasiveness, interwoven, tying up our being. Surely we would much rather have the divine vine twisting and surrounding every aspect of our soul instead. Where arrogance is found we can be sure that the softer places of pride are also nearby. And where pride dwells we can be certain fear still resides. Arrogance, pride, self-importance, and false humility are the places we protect within ourselves, the weaknesses we have yet to forgive and entrust to love's empowering oneness.

Pride blinds us to believing 'I' is more important than 'we', attaches us to self instead of opening us to the silence. Pride and sacredness are opposites. This is why the sacred presence demands so much of us to know its reality. We are called to empty ourselves, to turn ourselves inside out if necessary until we are empty of everything but the pure desire for what is within the silence.

As we become free of pride we are less afraid to feel what we truly desire, the great soul of souls in the uncreated wonder. As our pride decreases, our desires lessen, except for the one true desire that we really yearn for. The everyday human aspects of life guide us. Every time we are willing to risk more of ourselves, our pride is a little less secure. Taking risks affirms our vulnerability and keeps the silence close to us. When we let go of our concern about how others see us, our arrogance has less to stand upon. If our goal is to confront our most difficult problems and embrace our enemies, our pride is less in control. If we are willing to see the weaknesses in ourselves and the strengths in others, arrogance is kept at bay. Moreover, if we are willing to see the weaknesses in our own strengths and find strengths in our own weaknesses, our personalities would be easier to change. Arrogance has difficulty surviving as we practice forgiving what is difficult to forgive or finding a sense of humor in the most serious things. Arrogance, the subtle presence of pride, may persist. But its very persistence only signals how much we have yet to receive of the intense light, the most beautiful love of the silence.

Meanwhile, although it is difficult to know which desires are sincere and which are simply our way of avoiding intimacy with the love in the silence, we are called to be on watch for every desire that appears important and wants to be taken care of right away. Arrogance lives not only in the one large idea that everyone notices, but also in the small aspects of our personalities that take great comfort in going unnoticed. For example, we often criticize our leaders for their aggressiveness and the plans they make for us. However, our judgments about our leaders and our reluctance to offer something better can just be other forms of pride. Arrogance often seeks to be comfortable and is afraid of being noticed.

In religious life or worldly life arrogance can easily go unnoticed. No one but ourselves knows the motivation for our actions. Our intention may seem good to everyone, but we know and the silence knows what's inside our hearts. If we practice noticing how many demands we make on others or how many of our prayers are concerned about our own welfare, we may become aware of how much pride is still a part of our lives. Without the love of the silence we could live our entire lives in the prison of our own grandiosity and reach life's end unprepared for love's realms in the stillness. Fortunately, nearly all forms of pride melt not so much in confrontation but in the gentle arms of the peaceful quiet.

Fortunately, every soul willing to be as small and as beautiful as the little flowers will discover on the final day an easy drop to the ground of heaven.

How do we live with less pride? How do we find humility? Only inasmuch as the silence has entered our daily being, only inasmuch as we have cloistered the silence within us, can our pride accept the great peace and take refuge in the vast moments that know no boundaries, except those we bring to its infinite love.

TEMPTATIONS AND CHOICES

Because of our fear of vulnerability and because of the distance we maintain between ourselves and the love in the stillness, we remain blinded by pride or arrogance. Often we do not know how to handle all of life's choices and so we make those that are most self-serving. For example, it is much easier to find the energy to run our own errands than to find the same energy to respond to the errands our partner wants us to run. We are easily tempted to fulfill our own wishes first because for us they seem more important. Even with our own wishes we often do not know how to differentiate between opportunities for a better life and temptations that may give us immediate comfort but take us further from ourselves and the silence. In relationships, work, and social occasions we make many choices every day. Some choices support our interior life, adding to our growing intimacy with the quiet. Other choices may be impulsive, fearful reactions, or easy responses. Because of the noise and stress in our life, we are often tempted to make choices that only dull our senses and separate us from our true feelings and desires. For example, we may overeat, run across town for something we don't really need, react harshly to others, or engage in compulsive behavior. With the silence we could stop to make more conscientious choices. Our spiritual practice helps us become aware of our choices so that we choose a life that brings us closer to our inner selves and the silence.

The large temptations in life are like a job that promises many benefits but offers little personal fulfillment, a relationship we hold onto out of fear of being alone, or any path that feels untrue even though we follow it day after day. We can deal better with these temptations as we learn to resist life's small temptations. Every day we are tempted to make poor choices out of laziness, pressures from others, fears, or because of promises that sound good but that ultimately do not serve us. Some people encounter the same temptation again and again. Our choices either guide us toward finding more quiet spaces inside or pull us apart from our feelings and away from life about us. The choice we keep making in one form or another is to embrace or run from the silence.

Life's temptations are our daily distractions. Sometimes, as we become aware of the silence receiving us, we reach for something to distract our awareness, to dull our feelings. The love is so great and we may feel so unworthy. Almost every soul in one way or another settles for a life of distractions instead of a life full of silence.

The first step is to become aware of the unconscious moments during our day, the things we do routinely, almost automatically. Consciousness grows as we put more awareness into our choices and what we are doing.

The next step is to practice pausing, breathing a couple times, let's say, before ordering a second dessert. Instead of automatically turning on the radio we should ask ourselves why we are covering up the silence. What do we really want to be doing? When temptations become choices, awareness replaces automatic responses. Each moment of awareness includes the sacred silence. Routine behavior dulls our feelings, but conscious behavior involves the silence. Our pathway into silentness includes being aware of life's large and small pressures, suggestions, and seductions and taking more time to make better decisions. In our momentary pauses, the presence of silence has added to our being, giving us the freedom to choose the course to follow. At issue is not necessarily what we are doing but how aware we are of doing it. Eating a dessert quickly because it is there in front of us is quite different from choosing a dessert, eating it slowly, and enjoying it.

A wise priest once told a group I was with, "The greatest temptation is our discouragement. And our discouragement is just another form of pride." Temptations continue as long as there are parts of us that are left to be distracted, disconnected, or separated from the golden heart of silence. Until we disappear into the quiet realms completely, our distractions are gifts to remind us there is still more of ourselves to take "home" into the silence. And as we return "home" we should look at the fears that lead us into distractions. We are afraid of the immense love, so we settle for the little pleasures life offers. We are afraid of our insignificance in the great light, so we find little islands of pride and self-importance to stand upon. Our fears lead us into temptation and separateness. Without our fears, we would be simply with the still oneness.

We are called to an awareness where our ego does not dissolve into a void, into nothing as we may think, but surrenders to more and more awareness, which gives consciousness to the experience of our soul, alive in the light of the silence.

SELF-PITY AND AGGRESSION

The discouragement we encounter can easily lead to self-pity and aggression. Self-pity is one of the most effective means to deny the love in the silence. Of course the great presence cannot be completely eliminated from our lives. There is ultimately no defense to love. Self-pity, our moments of self-absorption, only last until we open again to others or allow nature to make room for the love that silence offers us.

Aggression is another means we have to stay separate from the silence. If excluded from our lives, the silence cannot focus or nourish our energy, so aggression seems to be the only way to get what we think we want. Whenever we resort to aggression to solve a problem or deal with a crisis, we are really saying we know of no better way. The peace, love, joy, and the other qualities of the silence are blocked from our perception. Aggression is a statement of our powerlessness. Pride has blocked our ability to find a better solution. Our moments of anger are the moments we exclude the presence of silence. Anger is energy that forms around the fear and hurt we are feeling. We react quickly, out of anger. In our love, in the conscious stillness, we can heal the fear and hurt. Whether losing our temper or continuing relationships that anger us, we are separate from our interior wisdom. We can bring our unconscious moments, our angry and hurtful self, to our meditations, hold them within our awareness, and invite the love of our greater being to help us care for our feelings.

Aggression is a cry for help. Many souls are crying for help to enjoy the fruits of the silence. Our aggression comes from relying on ourselves. The people we are angry with are really helping by pointing out our limits and returning us to the love in the gentle presence. Aggression comes from resisting the guidance that exists for us. Aggression is a sign of how helpless we are separated from the well of silence.

The intensity of our anger can teach us how much we desire the silence. The futility of our anger can lead us to see how powerless we are without a life of peaceful stillness. Anger, whether it comes suddenly and is gone or builds slowly and stays with us, can help us to take a new look at our independence from others, ourselves, and the silence. Anger in any form teaches us how much we look elsewhere and are disappointed with not finding the tenderness that is available for us in the unsounded world.

In the silence, everything is sacred, including our enemies. We are encouraged to carry them inside us with respect, for our enemies are giving themselves as teachers and guides from whom we can learn to depend upon the love of the silence.

Our struggles with each other are really struggles with the silence within us. The battles end as we remember that each confrontation is really between us and the vast presence. This is why with aggression there are no victories, no matter who is declared the winner.

INCONSISTENCIES

Anger or self-pity, the physical and emotional conflicts that keep us from centering in the silence, reflect our many inconsistencies. Our general intention may be to be loving, yet we continue to have feelings of impatience, jealousy, and resentment. The disparity between our intentions and our feelings is an example of our inconsistencies. They reflect our desire for a sacred life and our life distracted by noise. All monks and nuns become terrified at some point in their lives by how much peace they can know and how aggressive or discouraged they can feel, sometimes within moments of each other.

Inconsistencies are what the unsounded world exposes. We can pray for world peace but have trouble finding peace in our homes. We can be concerned with truth but find so many moments in the day when we are not truthful. We can talk about sharing with others in need only to discover how many possessions we have and how difficult it is for us to give to others. The closer we live to the care of the stillness, the more often we see our own inconsistencies. This is the price we pay for living so close to such tenderness. We are forced to see in the mirror of the silence our selfishness, short tempers, and persistent hardness toward others. The silence is very patient with those who live in love's path, who see their inconsistencies often and clearly. The stillness helps by making our contradictions so difficult to bear that we choose to live even more with the silence.

———————

Our inconsistencies are the distance that remains between our beliefs and our actions, our ideas and our feelings, the distance inside we have yet to fill with true peace and quiet. Imagine the day when our beliefs and actions, ideas and feelings, flow out of the same source. On this day we will be living in and with the sacredness of the all-encompassing.

———————

PATIENCE

Our inconsistencies can lead us to a new relationship with patience. Patience is one of the few requests that the love in the quiet makes of us. The silence can ask us to be more patient because the silence is patient waiting for each of us to decide to come "home" out of free will.

———————

The practice of patience in living, in having, in being relieved, in being waited upon, comforted, and fed, in dying, brings us much of the nature of silence itself. Patience teaches us to be less impulsive with our wishes and more open to the silence and a greater will for us. Patience watches as we wrestle with our emotions. Patience witnesses all our inner battles until we accept the peace in patience. We are invited to be patient in all things. Being patient in suffering lessens the pain and fear that it will last forever. Being patient in joy is not to be frantic that it may be ending but to really enjoy what is present instead. Patience prepares us for the heart of the quietude.

Patience with children, parents, friends, and work develops as we feel the depths of patience that the silence holds for us. Patience slows us down in the moments we are in a hurry, opens us to humility when we are tempted to insist upon our way. Patience can open us to feel how much the silence is already with us and how much our real needs are taken care of. Patience is not blind acceptance but conscious acceptance. Each act of patience is a step toward wholeness where we are not a victim of the events about us but feeling the inner harmony that is available.

The practice of being patient is a specific path to the silence. In our patience we join the love and timing of the silence. In our patience we are led into the will of the silentness, and life is not so busy and pressing. Patience allows doors to open to other experience while we are waiting. Patience leads us to greater harmony with life instead of just sitting. The moment we practice being patient we begin to be open for peace, wonder, and other feelings besides frustration.

RESISTANCE

Patience softens us to feel more of our interior being, helping us to be aware of our resistance to life, a life full of the perfection of silence. We often resist what is good for us out of habit. We may not know better. Our quest for wholeness is to help us become conscious of our resistance to having room inside of us for silence.

Resistance is saying no when saying yes would bring more love. Resistance is giving up or backing away when if, instead, we stood still or went forward, more light, more truth would enter a situation. Resistance is holding onto our problems instead of forgiving the people involved and trusting the care of the perfect presence. Resistance is staying where we are when we know there is love for us to receive and to give to others. Every time we rub against the silence there is our resistance and our willingness to join the love inside. Our resistance changes into willingness as we

invite the silence to be with us. As we include the quiet world
there is less and less to resist.

------

*Resistance to any person or experience is resistance
to a part of ourselves, since all parts of life are related
in the stillness. The love of the silence has brought this
person or experience to us. We are asked to love each
person, every experience, until all separation is brought
to an end. All the love in the silence is with us and
available to help us.*

As we overcome every resistance, love flows into our
hearts. The flow of the life force that draws from the silent
well inside us is increased. Love's unseen hosts in the
stillness are intimately involved with us, helping us to
forgive others and love the obstacles before us. The greater
the obstacle the more the love in the invisible realms will be
with us, if we do not resist.

A life of many obstacles can be a life representing the
silence in many attempts to bring fear home to the safety of
the pure presence. Every soul is called to follow the road
ahead as it enters conscious life. Many great souls bow
down to a life full of ordinary and extraordinary difficulties
not out of weakness or compromise but from conscious acceptance. These souls take on more for the silence. Meanwhile, inside these people the silence maintains such a strong
hold that nothing can shake it loose. The path of being
aware and overcoming our resistance can bring us fully into
the stillness. In our tensions and struggles are the awareness
and the joy to discover that we are not alone and that every
resistance we overcome is for all of us.

SUFFERING

Our resistance brings us to our suffering. The only
purpose for suffering is to find the place inside of no

suffering, where healing can occur. Our broken body and wounded personality have only one purpose, and this is to redirect us to the pure love of our soul, the place where real healing takes place. In the love of the silence all suffering is transformed into peace. Instead of ignoring suffering or trying to conquer it, we can let suffering guide us to a new place inside, a place where there is no suffering, only the unvoiced presence.

For the monk or mystic, suffering can present a distinct pathway into the silence. Pain surging through feelings in the body can lead us into the great body of silence. The naked body becomes the mystical body as we allow suffering to be our messenger, carrying us to the stillness. The very ill and dying show us the peace-filled love that comes from gradually accepting their vulnerability and nakedness. Their conscious surrender is not giving up but opening up to the peace inside them.

Suffering can persist when we try to be in two different places instead of simply being. For example, when ill we are tempted to be normally active when our bodies are expressing a need to be quiet and gentle. Pain can be the energy we are pushing in the direction of activity as our body pulls us to relax and slow down. Unresolved difficulties at work or with a partner can result in physical pain that seems to have no end. Pain can be the energy we are denying and our body is simply expressing the denial. Suffering has purpose as it leads us to ask where we are in the silence. Our suffering can slow us down to the silence where the inner harmony is present. The path of suffering can take us very far into the inner being where only the most pure love is found.

Suffering shows us our limits, our limits without the silence. Here the silence can teach love's limitlessness.

Suffering connects us with all beings who suffer and are sincerely looking for their place in the unsounded world.

Together we can learn to give shelter to the love of the silence, a home where the simple presence is welcome. Literally our place of pain can be the perfect spot where we learn to invite the most pure love in the quiet. In accepting our inconsistencies, the practice of patience, and our willingness to forgive our resistance, we build an internal structure to care for our pain. The monastery without walls is a full interior life that is open to all life experience, reminding us of its sacredness. Pain attracts our awareness. Instead of contracting, with awareness we can expand again as we feel the silence within us. As pain represents our separateness from the peace and quiet, our healing represents the wholeness the silence gives us. Our pain purifies our desire until only the true love is touching us. Conscious suffering can help build a conscious home inside for silence. Every place of discomfort becomes a new place where the pure presence is invited and welcomed.

The body's purpose is to take us through physical suffering to the silence where there is no body. Suffering can be part of the experience in achieving complete freedom. Our senses, feelings, and thoughts introduce us to the hidden joys and secret pleasures in the stillness that only the body can show us. Our soul carries the memory of our being made in the divine image. Thus no matter what circumstance we may be in, all the power of creation, all the love of the uncreated being, are with us and can transform any situation. No challenge, disability, or illness is greater than we are in the silence.

The traditional monastery can remind us that suffering, like joy and peace, has its role in life's many seasons. Having a broken body, an empty stomach, or a lonely heart can provide a pathway into the sacred silence. These times can impress upon us that anything less than a way of life in the silence is painful and unacceptable. These times can be heavy on our soul until we realize that a life that does not open to the soul

*is no longer true. As suffering brings new direction to
our lives and purification of our feelings, hopelessness
gives birth to the new life. In the monastery without
walls all suffering is held sacred. Now faith can lead us
to know the most intimate love, the peace of the silence.*

ILLNESS AND HEALING

In the monastery without walls every illness has its own
hidden path into the silence. Two people may have the same
illness, but the lessons and the path where the illness is
leading them may be different. First, by attracting our
attention, illness can turn us away from our normal routine.
Then, as we follow our course of healing, illness keeps
leading us on a path we wouldn't have otherwise known.
Unhealthy habits and many personal qualities may change
for the better. Friendships past and present may be seen
differently. Simplicity and forgiveness might become more
important. Gratitude for past good health may occur.
Through illness, peaceful feelings can become important
not only in our bodies but in many different parts of our
lives. As we follow our inner path, the pain and other signals
of the illness can lead us to greater depths and wider
horizons in the world of silence. Illness can make us sensitive
to our interior being and to life in general. Illness and healing
is where the love of the quietude and our bodies interface.

The body's subtle messages can lead us to the subtle
presence of the stillness. In illness, the simple presence slows
down that part of us that can no longer be busy. In illness the
silence rubs against our routines, our normal awareness,
until we respond and open to more of our being. We gain
wisdom in how to take better care of ourselves. Illness may
reflect our physical imbalance, poor diet, lack of exercise, or
frantic pace of life. Illness may represent the emotions we
have trouble accepting like anger, resentment, and guilt.
Illness can result from the accumulation of noise and stress
in our lives, which our bodies, fine instruments that they are,
can no longer tolerate. Our whole being is calling for the

pure sound in the silence. As the fine tone of stillness resonates in every part of us, illness draws our attention and calls us to accept more of ourselves. The silence is already present to help us.

Souls who carry a long, difficult illness frequently develop a special relationship with the silence. They become sensitive to the peace and the quiet in ways others never know. They discover that the painful moments decrease as they expand into the eternity of the silence. To embrace the love in the stillness is not to give up on life but exactly the opposite. As we live more in the present, the peace of the silence serves to make us feel more aware, more available, more alive for love. To embrace the quiet is neither to resign ourselves nor fight back. In fighting an illness, we can be fighting ourselves instead of aligning ourselves with the healing process. The body is hurting for acceptance and care, not additional conflict.

People who are ill are monks and mystics in disguise. Through living very close to their physical limits, their vulnerability opens their soul to these limits. Illness is full of opportunity to be less busy and more appreciative of simply being. Little things, such as a conversation or a walk, can lead to a world full of the intimacy of silence. We can resist where we are being led or we can see illness and healing as a time of living more fully with our sacred self. The discomfort pinning us down is pressing us to the silence. As we let go of our plans and our everyday identity, the silence can join us in a new life closer, new identity fuller of our true essence.

For the monk or mystic inside us the important question is not whether we should take certain medicines and how much. The question is whether we will use illness as an opportunity to live closer to the love in the silence. The doctor or the operation may represent the love in the silence that is specifically for us. Illness calls us to receive love whatever direction it comes from.

As our perception of illness changes, we realize all healing occurs in the silence no matter how much technology or medicine is involved. Sometimes the process of accepting treatment is a necessary teaching for us to receive care from others. The question might not be whether to use modern healing methods but whether we are committed to life full of sacred moments of silence, the sacredness our body is hurting for.

———

The specific part of the body that is ill can represent our need for silence. For example, athletes who hurt themselves are called to make peace with their bodies whether they can return to sports or not. Business people with heart problems who are usually too busy for their family and loved ones are literally being shown to value their hearts, including their relationships. People who cannot accept their anger may develop symptoms of stomachaches, headaches, even cancer. The denied anger their body is expressing is crying for the gentle acceptance available in the stillness. While waiting for the body to heal, the discomfort can represent a call into the silence. It can be imagined as an antenna receiving the love in the silence needed. The more intense the pain, the more important it is to give discomfort our attention while searching for the silence within it. Pain represents the contractions of our awareness, and through our meditations and prayer we expand again discovering how our interior being is much greater, the being that lasts long after the body is no longer with us. Any illness can be an opportunity to stop and feel the peace and quiet that is usually unnoticed and unappreciated. In the stillness are the peace and the love that heal.

———

Historically, in monasteries and cultures where there was a shortage of doctors and medicine, there were healers who were skilled in representing the silence. Symptoms were seen as the body's desire for love. Through the laying on of hands, rituals, and simply being present, the healer brought the love of the silence to the patient. We do not understand these skills from the viewpoint of our technology. But from the viewpoint of illness as a soul knocking impatiently on the door of life, healing and the monastery without walls have new meaning.

As illness expresses separation from life, the silence restores our connection to ourselves, to each other, and to the earth. When our will is limited, illness presents the opportunity to seek a greater will. When we are incapacitated we have a chance to trust further the capacity of the quiet places inside us. Healing can be the specific pathway into the silence our soul is seeking to lead us to. The breakdown of the physical body can lead us to building the spiritual body.

From the viewpoint of the silence, a well person is not necessarily healed just as an ill person can be quite well spiritually. In the silence only the light of the soul exists.

TEARS

During the times of tears the silence calls us to remember that our tears are more than small bodies of water. In each tear are the memory of innocence and the presence of the love in the silence.

There are tears of the parent and tears of the child, tears for others and tears for our own soul. There are tears of joy and tears of sadness, there are tears for future times that will not happen and tears for times forgotten. There are first tears and last tears, tears without ending. There are the tears for those who cannot cry and tears for those whose tears won't cease.

There are tears in the wind, the cold, and the sun, tears in company and tears alone in the night. There are tears over little things as well as over large ones. There are tears for children and old people—maybe because they are so close to their feelings and their tears. There are tears for everything in nature for which we are willing to feel, just as there are tears for every kind of pain and excitement. And the love in the quiet, like the perfect mother, knows exactly what we are crying for. There are tears for when we do not have enough and tears for when we have too much. Like many of the great saints, Saint Francis cried and cried. He was tearful when he found himself in the perfect joy of the silence and when he felt lost and far away from the silent beauty. The lives of the saints are lives of inspired silence. They can bring us to tears or make us wish for them. With tears, lives of heart-filled wonder have no endings but only new beginnings.

There are tears for all occasions and when there is no occasion and we just feel like crying. Tears are the blood of the soul. Crying is a sacred expression of the silence. And when the tears just will not stop or there is no reason for them to continue, it is important to remember that each tear is for all of us, especially for those without any.

Pray your tears never stop coming, that you find more and more wonder worth crying over. Perhaps for some souls it is true that the peak experience of God is in tears. For such a soul there simply are no more excuses not to cry.

DEATH

In the monastery without walls death is not something to be denied. It is only our last step into the silence. All the little deaths along the way, the loss of youth, jobs, relationships, and physical health are simply smaller steps in the same direction. As we practice giving ourselves to the quiet, death becomes less frightening. It is simply the final gift. When we finally give ourselves completely to the love in the silence, nothing is left to distract our attention. An immense love, an intense light, wait on the other side of our independence from the stillness. Relatives and friends who have completed the journey before us are waiting for the reunion. As the curtain of our separateness is lifted, the pure consciousness, our true wholeness, which we experience only occasionally in normal life, are present. We become aware of so many things, in so many dimensions at once. Instead of losing our body, which we spend so much energy fearing, we are finally gaining our body. But of course it is not a physical body we gain but the body of our soul. We have returned to the dimension where our wholeness is included and received. Unfortunately, most of us are not prepared for the transition that occurs at death. The sudden intensity of the experience of complete acceptance that is available at death can overwhelm us. Out of touch with our souls, our consciousness scrambles to understand and integrate what is happening or could be happening. Meanwhile, at death perhaps the most beautiful moments of our being are passing by and we are not prepared to enjoy the newly found peace without limits.

Our spiritual life prepares us for death's new beginning. Successfully detaching ourselves from our body, people, and environment depends upon how close we have become to the silence. Our spiritual body needs to practice "coming home" to the silence each day and letting everything go that keeps us busy and demands our attention. Whatever we feel connected to presents our reality. So how can death be a transition into the golden heart of the silence if we have never spent any time getting to know it during our lifespan on earth? Our soul needs to practice "keeping in touch" with the qualities of the great quiet, such as humility, forgiveness, peace, and love. This is why we need to feel complete with each day, each relationship, and each project of our life. Unresolved feelings over relationships from the past and continued preoccupation with wanting new things only distract our attention from the love and peace our souls in the perfect stillness have to offer. With the practice of being available for the love in the silence, death is simply the final act of becoming totally available for the supreme gentleness of the Intimate Being.

Death is our birth into the caring of the infinite stillness. Unless we practice feeling the inner quiet available now in the silence, we will not be prepared for such light and grace later on. Every time we are willing to let go of our physical and emotional entanglements and practice surrendering ourselves as if dying into the quiesence, our capacity to enjoy the caring quiet increases within us. We are preparing ourselves to receive the arms waiting to help us accept the silent beauty when we let go at the final separation.

Each time a soul crosses through the door to the other side some of the weights he or she has carried in life cross as well. Each person brings some of the separatedness, some of the noise of the world through the doorway to the immense light, the great wholeness in the quiet. Any suffering at death's doorstep is the gift that each soul has taken on to bring to the love of the silence. Suffering is the chance for purification. The noise of the world we carry inside us is being transformed to silence. The purification taking place is not only for that soul but also for all of us, for everything that is separate from the peaceful kingdom. After the final step and release, the joy-filled freedom comes soon enough. Every step into the final harmony is perfect, no matter how much unfinished business of this world remains.

We can never judge a soul's journey by the quality of his or her physical life. Only the pure heart in the silence knows the full details of our journeys. Many of the greatest souls in the stillness led the seemingly most ordinary human lives. But in their simple ways they were daily giving more of themselves to the workings of the love in the silence.

The kingdom of silence has its own perspective and modes of evaluating life as we know it. The life we take so seriously is simply an embryonic stage in relation to the vast life in the quietude. Death is but a moment before birth and the long journey ahead for the soul. Death is the final move out of our physical 'home' that has served our soul as a medium for certain experiences and learning processes we would not have gained otherwise. Here lies the great value of having a body and living in the physical sphere. The full value of having a physical body can be realized only as we stay connected to the source of life in the silence. Our dying is simply the contractions of the physical until we are released into spiritual realms. Because it is the love of the Mother that gives us our body, the love of the Father that gives us each breath, we can be assured that She and He will receive and guide us at the moment of death. The soul that lives for the silence, feels the support of the Mother and the Father to let go into the next phase of life. For such a soul this large step is hardly noticed when all the smaller deaths, life's losses and changes, have already been so thoroughly accepted.

———————

In the monastery without walls we return each stage of life to its sacred nature. Beginning with birth, every season of life calls for new respect and perspective of what is truly occurring. In cultures where the knowledge of the silence has disappeared, people have experienced unnecessary fears and traumas about death. Many of the ills in our bodies and society result from our desperate resistance to death. Our denial of death is part of the erosion of the silence. Our interior life remains hidden, hungry, underdeveloped, and unavailable. The unresolved fear of separation, the fear of death, only continues the experience of unnecessary separation. Those who allow themselves to feel the presence of death are opened to life with all its gifts and transitions. The monastery without walls serves all souls in transition. It is the experience of the sacred that helps us to go smiling into life's unknowns and particularly into the final night, which awakens the silence within us.

COURAGE

The monastery is the place of courage that gives us the faith to live life and every season fully. We have all the reason to be confident about what life brings to us, because the silence is the source of courage supporting us.

This courage is something we can draw upon at any time. It is a particular strength we can summon when moments before we felt unable. It seems the moment we reach toward our strength, not knowing whether it will be enough, we find courage, a greater strength joining us. Our being with the silence depends upon finding the courage to open, feel, and experience all sorts of things we never before imagined.

Courage comes from the perfect stillness. It is in the silence in the mountains and the forests. It lives in the quiet on the bottom of the oceans. Through every altar, the silence brings courage to us. There is no limit to the courage we can find, because the great awareness holds an infinite supply.

The monastery without walls includes the homeless, the poor, the people in jails and hospitals, the terminally sick, all the unwanted who help hold the courage for the silence. They are in the garden where the stillness plants courage to which we are all a witness. Despite the odds, their source of strength comes from feeling their home, the earth underneath them, and the simple courage that the silence keeps close to them in their heart.

Courage is the brick and mortar of the simple life. The silence in the deep forests, high mountains, and great oceans is the reservoir of courage available to everyone. Love's oneness teaches us to turn toward the silence to find the courage, in order to take the risks that life invites us to take.

THE MONASTERY

Because of the mystique surrounding monks and nuns in religious life, we forget that the divine is found not only through leading a religious life, but also through becoming more aware of the human aspects of our lives, our struggles, fears, loneliness, illnesses, and ultimately death. The great monks and nuns themselves lived where each day and each relationship were filled with the presence of silence. They set the tradition of making our most ordinary life holy simply because our lives are so ordinary. They lived in simplicity, because the silence called for their total participation. There was no time or need for working for many possessions or to be busy with lots of activities. Life was precious and full of a special urgency to feel the silentness and sweet love.

In our daily survival, fears, loneliness and emptiness; in letting go of self-importance, pride, and arrogance; in sorting through our temptations to find positive choices; in how we feel sorry for ourselves or react to others; in how we come to terms with our inconsistencies and discover our patience and resistance; and in how we suffer, become ill, heal ourselves, and die—we open to how much we are really alive and full of the love of the silence. The monastery without walls reaches over the walls we have built in life, reminding us that more is present. Depending on how present we are, the walls about us no longer merely represent our human limits, but also serve to remind us to go farther, to explore the great silence.

CHAPTER EIGHT

FURTHER SPIRITUAL PRACTICE

The monastery without walls provides a place for life's sacredness and life's shadow, our everyday joys and challenges. The treasure in the stillness is found side by side and often within the negative experiences we encounter. It is our daily spiritual practice that guides us. It is in our daily spiritual practice that the silence weaves its golden threads through our entire being.

Everything we do out of love binds us closer to all beings and the silence. Any spiritual practice that does not come from love, no matter how popular or accepted it might be, has trouble finding a friend in the intimate quiet. If we are motivated by friendship, success, power, or anything other than love, then our spiritual practice may reap these things but not silence.

Every religion gives clear pathways into the pure stillness. The question is not whether we should favor a particular religion over another, but how much devotion and love we bring to the path before us. There are always reasons to reject a certain religion. However, we must be careful not to confuse the religious institution with the spirit in the silence. The world's great religions provide many paths that are well lit and traveled. For example, some churches are more intellectual while others are more contemplative. It is not which path we finally take into the silence but our commitment to find the love at the heart of the quiet that is important.

SPIRITUAL VOWS

In the monastery, spiritual vows guide monks and nuns through the dark passages around their souls to the many gifts that their union with the silence gives. Their spiritual vows create the marriage, the bond between the heart of the stillness and life's daily choices. As monks and nuns discover the silence through their commitment to their community, we can discover the richness of silence through our commitment to our partner and family. Regardless of form, every union shares the same potential reward of being together in the silence and the same temptation to separate when the peaceful silence is broken and feels far away. The making and practice of spiritual vows can serve to guide us into communion with the perfect silence. In difficult times monks and nuns are tempted to think about leaving or joining another community as married partners are tempted to think that freedom or a new partner would be easier and perhaps a better choice. Remembering our spiritual vows can help us face these times when we feel our community or partner has come between us and the silence. Our spiritual vows can help us find the humility to ask for the help and kindnesses we seek.

Our relationships reflect our interior life, our life with the silence. No brother or sister, partner or child, can give us what we are not willing to give ourselves. The answers we seek are ultimately within us and the silence. Remembering our spiritual vows can support us to stop and feel the gentle strokes of the silence. The commitment to our vows can help us get through the difficulty before us as we remember past challenges that now are gone. Marriage vows, whether with a partner or in monastic life, are not something we make once and then hope that they will endure. A spiritual vow is like a seal that enables us to grow closer and stay connected to the peaceful presence in life. Every day there is something new to love in our community or partner. Every day gives the silence an opportunity to show us a new face in those we live with. As husband and wife or as religious in community, we do not focus on the possible shortcomings of each other, but find in each other a bastion of love and support in the silence. Assuming this great responsibility allows the love of the quiet to be very close, in those about us. Our partner and our community become our best friend, lover, and places of refuge in the silence. We are the manifestations of the silence. As we recognize the monk and mystic in ourselves and each other, our spiritual vows continue to make our relationships just that much more sacred.

Spiritual vows have been tested through the centuries. Each vow guides our life to the life of our soul. Each vow tunes us to the heart of hearts, the silent place where only love waits to receive us.

POVERTY

The spiritual vow of poverty has guided Christian and Buddhist monks and mystics through the ages. In Hinduism, this vow is called the path of emptiness. A life of detachment makes life available for the love and truth of the silence. Living not merely for possessions is the key to living with life's real riches. In the East and West, wise beings have discovered through the ages that holding onto what little we have is to deny all that can be with us. If we spend our lives struggling for fantasies of gold, we will miss the golden heart of silence that is present for us.

The path of poverty is perhaps one of the most misunderstood ways to seek the perfect presence. Rich or poor we all have possessions, whether a large house or the shirt on our back. The question is how much of our lives should be spent pursuing or struggling over possessions. How strongly do we greed for more or seek fame instead of finding peace in our own depths of being? The path of poverty is a process of increasing our faith. Daily we are given the choice of either putting our faith in the life we have before us, forgetting today's blessings and worrying instead about tomorrow. Daily we can store away what we have or give as much of ourselves as we can, knowing that the silence is the great provider. The vow of poverty reminds us daily that the riches of the peace-filled quiet are our true source of wealth.

The vow of poverty does not mean being poor but exactly the opposite. Our poverty, our emptiness, is to make each day, every meal, our friends, and the possessions we enjoy more appreciated and not taken for granted. We discover on the path of poverty, or emptiness, that nothing we have is "ours." Everything is given as a gift. What is before us today may be gone tomorrow. So in the name of sacred poverty we give thanks and enjoy life's riches, which are among us. If we are free from the struggle for possessions, then the earth, the moon, and the stars are ours to enjoy. Instead of focusing on our small world of possessions, the whole world becomes available to enjoy.

The vow of poverty is not about suffering but about witnessing the substitutions for pure joy we attach ourselves to and settle for. As we feel our equality and dependence upon all living creatures, the spiritual life of poverty gives nothing less than the full life of the tenderness of the quietude.

We are called to follow the path of poverty as the way to remain focused on love's abundance in the silence. Each day we are given choices. Do we enjoy the moment or are we too busy accumulating things for another time? Are we living simply with the stillness close to us or are we possessed by life's everyday distractions? Are we too proud to apologize for our mistakes and forgive others for theirs or can we give up our self-importance to be with the silence? How poor or empty must we be before we are willing to admit that we are without the love of the great presence? The abundance of our interior world is revealed inasmuch we are willing to discover our true poverty.

It may be impossible to practice the vow of poverty living in such an abundant culture. The abundance we have around us can easily distract us and blind us from the physical poverty of the vast majority of the world's people. The abundance we live in can easily be used to hide in, to give temporary comfort to our spiritual poverty, our fears and human nakedness. This abundance can keep us needing and seeking more possessions to keep up with our neighbors. In an abundant culture how do we live in the spirit of poverty? How do we find the pure, simple peace when so many things call for our attention? The spirit of poverty means not taking for granted the life we are given every day. The spirit of poverty invites our sincere appreciation of all the riches, including the love we have in our lives. It is through conscious appreciation that we can gain awareness. The more awareness we give to the home that shelters us, the heat that comforts us, the machines that make life easier, the food that nourishes us, the more we can be true to our vow of poverty. To be poor in spirit is to find value in life's common occurrences, to be conscious of how much we have, how much love is with us to care for our human vulnerability.

CHASTITY

The second vow that Christian monks and nuns traditionally take is chastity. Chastity is the vow in which perfect love and our need for love interact. Chastity offers the goal of pure love. Simply keeping this goal in our hearts gives many golden moments.

Chastity, like poverty, must extend through every level from attitude to action. Chastity is the love that in relationships is experienced as brotherhood, that in action is experienced as forgiveness. Chastity is the purity, the white pearl that can fill our lives and take us freely far into the unspoiled awareness.

In areas of the East the desire for chastity is called the path of right intention. Everywhere chastity is part of the mystery of romance in which we desire love's purity only to find that we can neither possess the object of our love nor give up on our desire. Chastity is not the same as celibacy, although chastity may include it.

Many people are critical of the vow of chastity because of the implied celibacy. But the real issue is finding a way that yields the white snow of the stillness inside us. A sexual partnership does not satisfy our desire to be united with love. Love cannot be possessed. A very active sexual life may only serve to stir up our desires, keeping us separate from the love in the quiet that is already present. Attempts to be nonsexual can lead to the same result if it emphasizes sexual denial. Each being must find the true relationship with his or her own sexuality, which is the physical life force coming from the silence into physical being. Sexuality cannot be separated from the silence because the silence and love are interwoven. Certainly sexuality satisfies momentarily and yet intensifies our desires, including our desire for pure love, for chastity. Sexuality connected to fidelity can keep us in touch with God in our partner or God in our community. Through the discipline of fidelity, instead of looking for someone new to love whenever our current partnership is difficult, we give more of ourselves to the silence in ourselves and each other. Chastity is a call for service

where our faithfulness can give the possibility of beautiful wholeness. This wholeness includes the experience of solitude in relationship and the fulfillment of desire that comes from experiences of shared silence. Between us and our partner is the love in the stillness. Within each of us is silence. The simple presence finds its true home as we invite it into the depths of our sexuality, our most personal needs, desires, wants, and will. Here we develop the relationship between our desire for love and God's desire for us that resides in the oneness. Here we discover the mystery of selfishness and selflessness coming from the same pure heart, the heart of chastity.

By avoiding sexuality, traditional nuns and monks can deny part of their wholeness in the silence. Yet for many, excluding sexuality can force them to express their energies and creativity in other ways, leading to a greater path of wholeness. As the traditional monastery can lead to denial, the monastery without walls can lead to excess. Either course leads us away from chastity. Chastity, the simple purity of being in the silence, is not merely a rule that we either follow or don't. Neither rigorous discipline nor carefree spontaneity tames the emotions for the still place inside. The prayerful life committed to chastity carves our emotions into a shining bowl for the soul. The vow of chastity discloses how dependent we are upon learning to receive the love in the quiet, if we want to become conscious and steadfast in this love.

As the vow of poverty reminds us there is really nothing to hold onto and that we should continually seek the silence, the vow of chastity reminds us to keep our path directed toward the most pure love and quality of living. Chastity is a practical spiritual guide

that keeps our lives simple and helps us to seek the most
clear way that is honest and true.

Of course true poverty or chastity is not something
we can accomplish by ourselves. We hold the inten-
tion. We make the daily decisions that keep us heading
in the right direction. The simple presence supports
and rewards us with spiritual poverty and chastity as
we bring our physical and emotional lives to the silence
for the help and care we need.

Chastity is the path of giving ourselves to the purity of the
silence in everyone. Chastity gives us the faithfulness to seek
the silence in all we do, all we meet. Like all vows, chastity
is a gift from the silence where the love inside can show itself.

OBEDIENCE

Vows or sacred promises to God in a partner or God in
a community raise our fear of surrender. We rebel. We
submit. We confront and we give in. The vow of obedience
is the commitment to find the true authority, the authority
of love within us and everyone.

As with poverty and chastity, the vow of obedience
is often criticized and rarely understood. As poverty is
the promise to be spiritually poor so as to be empty and
available for the wonders of the quietude, and as
chastity is the sincere intention for relationships that
are simple and true so as not to delute love's silent
beauty, obedience is being attentive to love's will, the
inner truth we find from knowing the perfect presence.
Obedience is a call to vulnerability where we can be in
touch with what is real and important.

Obedience is the path that offers freedom from our greed, laziness, and other personal traits that do not ultimately serve us. In areas of the East the student surrenders all will to the master. In the West the monk or nun gives up self-interest in order to be the servant of the community, the servant of God's will. As poverty raises the question of how many possessions are too many and chastity raises the question of when love is selfish need and when love is truly for another, obedience helps us question our will and the higher will in the stillness. Vows are to help us to live in the world's seeming contradictions so that we can grow nearer to the quiet.

The vows of poverty, chastity, and obedience do not require us to live in traditional religious communities. In Christianity, vows are taken temporarily for several years and then made for an entire lifetime. But in Buddhism it is common for people to take religious vows for a few years and then return to worldly life. Wherever we are, the world around us can serve as our monastery. In taking the vow of obedience we intend to live a life that is true and simple. Obedience is the vow to listen to a greater calling, the calling from the silence, and to adjust our will to a greater will, the divine will. On this path, because we do not have a superior or teacher from whom to learn the art of surrendering to the silence, we must trust the oneness directly as it becomes known to us. We find our capacity to trust as we develop our spiritual practice. As our daily schedule and goals center around a common purpose of sacred silence, our inner voice is less conflicted and becomes more clear and direct. As our life flows more in one direction, the still voice inside, our conscience, our intuitive being, can guide and protect us. With our commitment to living the truth, the silence gains priority in our lives and guides our willpower to where our will and the higher will are the same, to where we have attuned ourselves to our highest purpose.

The vow of obedience invites the lucid presence into our everyday lives so that we can make decisions that will express our wholeness. Obedience means asking the wisdom of the silence to be in charge instead of our own changing and limited ideas of what we think is best. Obedience to the silence within us helps us to sort out which decisions result from fear, insecurity, or need and which decisions come from the abundance of love and compassion. Obedience establishes the reign of the peace-filled quiet and the simple love in every corner, every room, every small part of us. Obedience calls us to pursue the most love-filled life, to risk and trust our way into the most love-rich moments. Obedience reminds us that life is more than being self-sufficient. We are called to an open life, to give up our need to control when it severs us from the sacred life. Our work, relationships, activities, and prayers—everything is under the guidance of our commitment to pursue love in its purest, the heartful life in the silence. The monastic part of us feels called to a life where our physical, emotional, intellectual, and spiritual being must come from the true place of love in the silentness. Worn close to our heart, our vows are like the undergarments we wear in daily life. They are the clothing for our soul, representing the love in the perfect quiet in our noise-filled world. A life of obedience is a life of responsibility, forgiving all wrong authority from the past, knowing the right authority by testing the results. Obedience places our mind in alignment with our life of emptiness, our heart of pure desire.

Poverty is the empty boat I offer for whomever, whatever, the silent love gives to journey with me. Chastity is the white sail, the pure desire, for a life that is simple and true. I hold the sail tightly to my chest, trusting the wind of higher destiny to take me to the most pure place. Chastity is the sacred life I long to remember from the silent-filled being of my soul. Obedience is the commitment I make to feel and honor my soul, the soul of souls in the stillness above all else. I vow to risk sailing into the intimacy where only love is calling me.

CHARITY

Some traditional nuns and monks who have felt called from the walls of the monastery have taken another vow: the vow of charity. Mother Teresa of Calcutta is the most well known. Inspired by her, many people in religious orders and outside are using the vow of charity to guide them and to give meaning to their life in the modern world.

This is the vow of service to the poorest of the poor. Some take this vow out of gratitude for the opportunity to take the vows of poverty, chastity, and obedience. The love is so intense that only another vow, the vow of charity, can help them express their thankfulness. The vow of charity is to serve God in all forms, to live with love in action.

A life given to charity is a life truly given away. And a life that is truly surrendered to serving is a life that has placed no obstacles between itself and the silence. So the nun and the monk who take the vow of charity quickly realize they are being given even more in their desire to live a life for others, for the unvoiced love everywhere.

Service to the poorest of the poor is to keep our eyes, ears, and heart on the silence, which is always present. For the poor, the most naked before us, who must face life's ever-present vulnerability, the silence is very near. The commitment of service to the poorest of the poor is a commitment to remain very close and dear to the pure presence in whatever disguise. The vow of charity is a spiritual and yet practical vow to give when it is difficult to give, to find time to listen when we want to speak. Charity is doing little things for others until we learn that it is a part of ourselves that we are serving. Charity simply asks us right now to reach out to the poor and the hungry, the naked place in others and ourselves. As we become aware of the silent-filled heart calling us, we respond with love and care.

The vow of charity, giving to the poorest of the poor, teaches us the gift of giving. In our spiritual practice, the vow of charity supports and guides us to live a life in the golden silence with those who are needy, in a world that so often is seeking self-satisfaction. The workings of charity reveal very much about the silence and the essence of service in which love given away is purified and received.

Charity is not how much we give but the quality of love in our giving. Charity is being more involved in the small ways of loving in life. Charity begins at home by loving our family and the people close to us. Charity continues in serving the poor who hunger for the piece of bread that nourishes the body and the soul, the poor in heart who hunger maybe just for a smile. Charity is meeting the great longing for affection felt by so many, the need simply to have someone to talk to. Perhaps like no other vow, charity draws us closer to the heart of the stillness because we have to continuously receive from the divine heart to find the love that is worth giving.

MARRIAGE VOWS

As the vows of poverty, chastity, obedience, and charity open us to the presence of the silence about us and the sacred life, marriage vows carry the same opportunity. Historically, marriage vows have been the primary means to protect us from wandering astray and preserve the sacredness of creation. The vows begin by expressing the holiness of two souls united in marriage. They grow in meaning as married life faces the challenges of opening to silence. Today, however, so many committed relationships have come to be little more than contracts, which people outgrow and change. The breaking apart of so many marriages is symbolic of the loss of the sacred in so much of modern life.

The monastery without walls serves to honor and protect the vows of marriage. Marriage is the commitment two people make to discover the silence in each other, in good times and bad, in every season, in all of life. Marriage is the commitment two people make to discover the silence, to explore the silence together. We can change partners, but the challenge to find communion with the silence never ends. Finding the unending oneness in every mood and circumstance, finding more love of the quiet in easy times as well as in the challenging ones, are the real gifts of marriage. The love between two souls can enable them to receive the holiness of the silence in the most simple and ordinary daily routines. Marriage is the sacred bond of silence that two people can return to again and again for the support they need to live a life full of the golden awareness.

When two souls agree to step together into the unknown and help each other face their loneliness and fears, they find many blessings in the silence to support them. The vast presence offers marriage as a shelter to protect them. Marriage is the pathway on which two souls join to surrender to the all encompassing love.

Marriage invites the peace-filled life where every struggle, every joy, every disappointment, loves lost and found, are brought to the love in each partner, in the silence. In marriage a love that diminishes expects too much from the partner and does not trust enough while searching for the heart of the stillness. Marriage is love in action, in service to our partner. Loving service without expectation leads to the pure place of silence in each other. Partners in a marriage, whose goal is to be free of large expectations, are free of large disappointments, are full of personal responsibility, and are thankful for having someone to share the silence with. So many people in relationships spend their time trying to change each other, looking for what only an intense spiritual life can offer, the perfect love of the silence.

Marriage is never the source of our problems or the source of our answers. It is each soul choosing to receive or struggle with the love in the silence in himself or herself, in each other, and in life. As we open ourselves to the endless presence we sometimes think that our partner is our problem, our enemy. At other times our partner is the only one to help us, our savior. But our partner is merely our partner on the great path into the silence. Marriage is the special bond, held sacred in the quiet, for two souls to discover together love's beauty and great mystery.

As the religious are called to love God even when their prayers have gone dry and they don't feel any comfort from the silent presence, we are called to love our partner when our relationship has become dry and we are receiving little or nothing from the other. These times, when there is seemingly no return for our efforts, are turning points in the development of our soul, our commitment to love for love itself. These times that we love through our hurt and disappointment are the times that the presence of silence is taking a greater hold of us and our personality is letting go for something greater . . . love. The perfect love two souls can inspire in each other, withdraw from each other, is taking the place of doubt and fear.

PERSONAL VOWS

In addition to the traditional vows of poverty, chastity, obedience, charity, and marriage, people can take personal vows. Such vows can give us direction in everyday life so that we can affirm our desire to live in the monastery without walls. Anyone can take personal vows to value, honor and be with the silence. Traditional vows of poverty, chastity, obedience, charity, and marriage have stood the test of time, and many ordinary souls have become saints fulfilling them.

In normal life there is no one to judge or hold us accountable for the promises we make, nothing other than the truth, the mirror in the simple quiet. People are taking their own personal vows during weekend retreats, for months, even years at a time. Vows of simplicity, forgiveness, and gratitude have a clear way of guiding everyday life. Each day is planned, spent, and reflected upon in simplicity, forgiveness, and gratitude no matter how the day passes. Vows of peace, love, innocence, or purity remind us that we can find a truer relationship in all things. Vows of grace or joy help set the tone for each day so that we can be open for grace and joy in all situations. Vows of acceptance or surrender can remind us that all our experiences are interwoven into the fabric of the silence.

There are many possible vows, each bringing another quality of the love in the stillness into everyday life. There are vows of strength and courage, which include the strength to be also weak and the courage to be also humble. There are vows of compassion and gentleness, which encourage softness in everyday life. Vows of prayer and devotion remind us that every aspect of the day is to be reflected upon in prayer. The vow of perfect joy is to seek the joy in all experiences, even the most difficult.

When choosing personal vows we must not choose qualities of love we think we should have or need. Spiritual vows are gifts from the silence. By taking a vow for however long, we are affirming our participation in the quiet. Each vow affirms our commitment to live life as a gift, as a sacrament.

Vows that continue to touch our soul come from the place of our deepest desire. If we could have the quality of love we want most from the silence, what would we choose? Peace? Love? The vow of peace or love means to practice experiencing daily the peace or love of the stillness in every circumstance. We make a conscious effort for each interaction to be one of love. Or we make a conscious effort of being available for peace in the day's many small moments. If we could have anything we desired from the silence, what would it be? Faith? Goodness: the ability to find goodness in everything, everyone? Taking these vows also means the daily practice of realizing the gifts we are willing to ask for: faith and goodness.

There are many qualities of silence we could make a promise to notice and to be aware of. Of course promises or vows have value inasmuch as we respect and honor where they lead us.

All vows should be taken slowly and felt until a clear yes comes from the depths of the silence within our hearts. Once this clarity comes, the vow helps build a clear, consistent path into the depths of love's being within us.

Monastic vows often are taken three at a time. In everyday life, three vows have a special presence. Whether they are traditional vows of poverty, chastity, and obedience or vows of peace, forgiveness, and gratitude, each vow adds a special perspective to the day and to our experience. Including the vows of peace, forgiveness, and gratitude each day strengthens us. Vows of love, compassion, and acceptance give life a specific flavor. Each vow is so powerful that it must clearly come from our own depths and be right in order to be of real value. Each vow should be practiced for a few days and then longer until it becomes clearly the right choice.

Vows have a way of leading us to the exact place in the silence where we desire to be. At the same time they protect our vulnerability as we lead a silent life. People who sincerely want more solitude can take a vow of solitude and find it in many of their everyday activities. People who hunger for honesty from others can take a vow of honesty for themselves and be surprised at the results. Others who long for a feeling of reverence in their lives can simply take this as a vow. Before long they find themselves having reverence for their families, friends, brief moments in nature, their feelings, even their difficulties. Vows can provide the necessary structure to maintain the monastery without walls with its purpose. Each vow keeps us aware of a special part of the silence so that more of the veiled harmony becomes apparent. As marriage vows remind a couple that they are united in the love of the silence, personal vows remind us that we are not limited by the noise of the world but that we are participating in the mysteries of the created and uncreated being within us.

MYSTERIES

The silence is full of mysteries. There are the mysteries in the Bible's miracles. And there are mysteries that the great mystics talk about. There are mysteries in the discoveries of everyday life. Wherever love is present, the power and the vulnerability of love are a mystery. Wherever love prevails, the beautiful simplicity and glow of love's glory are a mystery.

Some mysteries are talked about and studied, but every mystery takes on meaning only as we participate in it. The mysteries of the silence take place in the most simple moments, beginning with the fresh air at dawn and ending with the starry skies at night. Each mystery is an expression of the silence designed to free us from the bonds of "normal" reality. As we give ourselves completely to this moment, our breath belongs not to us but to the perfect presence. Each day we give more of ourselves to the love in the silence until there is nothing left but intimate quiet. At this point the mysteries become our life as we become part of the body of the silence participating in the great mysteries.

The mysteries invite us to see the holy family in Christianity in our own family. The mysteries invite us to see the life and peacefulness of Buddha within our own life. The miracles talked about in all religions are evidence of the reality of miracles that can take place in our own life as we open to the mystery they represent. To this day the ancient mysteries, like the freeing of the Hebrews from the powerful pharaoh, or Christ providing fish and loaves for the multitudes, continue to pull at our restraints, stubborn beliefs, and lack of faith. Season after season the biblical stories take our personal lives and make them universal again as they truly are. Everything separate is reminded that we are joined. The mystery includes how each of our personal lives is interwoven into the life of all beings and love's will in the silence. The mysteries have no beginning or end but are given for us to participate with until the noise we live in disappears. In all its passion, the sacred silence is inseparable, full of mystery, and within us.

FASTING

Traditionally, fasting has been an act of purification. Nuns and monks refrain from eating while increasing prayer and meditation. They see fasting as an opportunity to be more in touch with the hunger of the soul. So nuns and monks fast for one day or as many as forty days especially during the holy season of Lent, so that they can receive the gifts of the silence. Fasting is the ageless practice of going without food to live intimately with the peace-filled quiet. As we practice not eating we become aware of the other things we do automatically that keep us away from our feelings and the silence.

In the monastery without walls many of our daily activities occupy places of importance that could be better given to pure silence. In addition to eating more food than is necessary, we make wasteful purchases, watch too much television, and indulge in other passive forms of entertainment and consumption that we do not really need. As a spiritual practice, we can become more accessible to the silence as we fast from those activities we do out of habit or because we can find nothing else to do. To stop watching television merely to read crime stories does not necessarily serve us. But if we stop watching television for an hour each day and meditate and pray instead, we have taken another step toward making the monk or mystic inside us a priority in our lives. Stopping any routine or habit temporarily or permanently and replacing it with a regular period of silence releases the noise of our personality to the peace of our soul. We are what we eat, do, and think, and how we spend our day. The interior life is strengthened as we discover how many everyday desires are fulfilled in the quiet, how many of our needs are satisfied in the perfect stillness.

Some of us, however, try to fast in order to quicken the spiritual process. Whether we fast from eating meat or food one day a week, from smoking or purchasing unnecessary things, fasting whose motivation is to quicken spiritual development, skip a step in the process, or impress ourselves or others yields limited results. Fasting to increase our attention toward the love of the silence and to appreciate the quiet presence can remove the fear and guilt that makes us attach ourselves to things instead of silence. Fasting to prove self-discipline or self-importance, fasting to suffer or to quickly change our lives, have limited effect. We can be simply substituting one compulsive behavior for another, compulsive fasting. But fasting to intensify our experience, to purify the noise within us, and to find a true place inside can bring the qualities of silence to the forefront of our awareness. Fasting can show us the parts of our lives that are distracted as we bring more of ourselves to the love in the silentness.

SACRED MUSIC, SACRED JOURNEYS

In addition to letting go of the parts of our lives that do not lead us to the silence, we can find pleasures to cultivate that serve to remind us of the pure love, the presence of our souls in the lucid presence. With so much noise in our lives we can forget the tone, the experience of pure sound. We can forget that there is an alternative to noise. Today most music comes from studios; the sound is produced and filtered over and over again. Sacred music comes from the hearts and voices of those who have committed themselves to knowing the true sound of the great quiet. In the depths and sincerity of their commitment sacredness is given sound. Classical music, Gregorian chants and music from Taize, many monasteries, and committed individuals in the moments of feeling their hunger for the divine have given us inspired sound. Sacred music through its simple purity heals the noise within us. The angelic notes resonate with the clear sound found in the silence, the sound where no part of us is excluded, where our entire being is welcomed and sung to.

As sacred music can remind us of the pure sound, sacred journeys can reawaken our respect for the earth and our journey on it. Pilgrimages to holy places like Assisi, Jerusalem, parts of Tibet, India, and many other places around the world can be conscious journeys where prayer, meditation, and the intention of creating a new more sacred life provide a structure to increase awareness. A sacred journey is travel with a purpose. Different from a vacation or any other kind of trip, pilgrimages are a very old form of spiritual transformation where the journey and all the little moments of travel are consciously used to bring us closer to our essential self. Times waiting in lines are spent in patience of the divine. Times eating are enjoyed as if receiving nourishment for the soul and the body. Times packing and unpacking, walking, visiting, and resting all have the single purpose of reawakening us to a fresh relationship with the silence and therefore a new relationship with everyday life.

TIME

The monastery without walls becomes better defined by how we spend our time. The more our time is spent with conscious purpose, the more we are directing our energies to rebuilding the sense of sacredness to our life. Reforming our life-styles so that they include more private moments, more time in nature, more time with our partners and children, and more time in meditation and prayer helps discover the sacred wherever we are.

Our relationship with the sacred requires us to have a new relationship with time: our days, weeks, months, and years. Time is more than something to organize and plan. Time is a gift from the silence. Inside the stillness there is no time because all is present. Past and future begin again as we separate ourselves from the vast presence. Time teaches us how valuable, brief, and precious time is. To become aware of time is to become aware of the many gifts of the moment. Each moment in the silence is an instant of eternity. There is a spiritual practice of gaining awareness of time, its time-lessness, its timeliness. Life enjoyed in present time can pass all too quickly, the time for prayer and the time for simply being is never enough. Eternity is found as we let go of the temptation to live in the past and future and find ordinary time to be filled with the presence of many sweet moments.

DISCIPLINE

The preciousness of time makes us want to find the discipline to organize and plan life to the fullest so that it does not pass us by. With discipline we can create a time for daily meditation and prayer, friends and nature, work and relaxation. With discipline we make our spirituality the foundation of our feelings, activities, and relationships.

Many of us hear the word discipline and think of punishment. We cannot separate the use of discipline as punishment from the use of discipline as a program for training and development. As long as we think of discipline as punishment we cannot open to our soul's need for consistency and commitment. For many to whom religious school was a requirement, feeling almost like a punishment, finding the personal discipline to build a sound and solid spiritual practice is difficult.

As disciples we are called to find spiritual discipline especially in the monastery without walls, where there is no teacher to remind and challenge us, to structure our path. We must find the inner discipline to make the life of our soul the priority for our being. We are called to find the discipline that is not a punishment but gives the everyday opportunity to realize our spiritual potential. It is the individual discipline we create for ourselves that carries us through the difficult times to new depths of our being and through the joyful times to even greater joy.

REPENTANCE AND PRAISE

Repentance and praise are two spiritual practices that are seldom embraced in modern spiritual life. But for the sincere heart, repentance for the times we deny the silent presence of love leads to fresh praise of life's unspoken wonders.

Repentance genuinely felt is as a new stroke of love for the heart, a fresh start for the mind troubled over the past. The words "I'm sorry" can say so much in a noise-filled world. Saying "I'm sorry" brings our attention to the moment. The noise around and within us stops, and the presence of silence once again can enter our relationships. Repentance as it flows from the self (instead of from the expectations of others) relieves the burdened life, now ready again for praise.

Praise is the natural state of a soul opened to the silence. Life is full of opportunities for praise. We can praise the silence in people's faces, the perfect stillness found in nature, the presence of the sun and the moon. We can praise everything that gives witness to the beauty of the quietude. And of course we can praise love directly in all the forms that we know love. Praise is one of the childlike emotions that wise old men and women in nearly every culture come to appreciate.

Sincere repentance and praise touch the noise we live with once again with the silent purity of our hearts. Repentance and praise both enlarge our lives, making more room for our souls and the silent presence that gives life its meaning.

SOLITUDE

Solitude is perhaps the mainstay of traditional monasteries. For some, only within the walls of the monastery can inner solitude find safety from a world driven by noise. Life in the noise-filled world is tested in how we find the time for solitude and how we use solitude to increase awareness of our being in the silence.

Solitude and silence give serenity, the quiet wisdom that knows wholeness however events are turning around us.

Solitude is in the hours and days set aside specifically for prayer and meditation. Solitude is not, however, necessarily the absence of company but merely those times we take for the absorption of silence. In fact, shared solitude, being together in the simple presence, can yield exquisite inner peace. Being alone does not guarantee solitude any more than being with others precludes solitude. Solitude can be found discovering how much we are not alone, how much the wind, the birds, the flowers, and the trees are with us. Solitude can lead us to discover how much we are connected with each other and all of nature. As we stand still inside, we feel, see, and listen more. Whether alone at the altar or on a busy street, solitude is the practice of noticing the simple moments and where they lead us. Solitude can expand our attention so that we can see how our breath is in rhythm with our thoughts and our thoughts are more in touch with our breath. The experience of solitude comes as our actions and our need to accomplish soften into more awareness. As we involve more awareness of our senses, the mind is more present for the gifts of solitude. The peace of solitude is the wholeness we can feel in the midst of any activity. The challenge is to find access to our peace, our simple being, in whatever we are doing, no matter how much we have to do.

Solitude is a way of life. We cannot have an empty mind for the stillness when our minds are always preoccupied with other things. Emptying our minds and stopping the unnecessary thoughts require our commitment to the presence in the silence. The mind stops for the perfection of the moment as we give the simplicity of the moment priority over the other things we pursue and spend time thinking about. The mind stops for silence as our fears are befriended in solitude. Solitude is the life we create for ourselves with the presence of timeless moments one after another.

DREAMS

Solitude for many is found only at night. Solitude can be the moments before going to sleep and after waking up. Solitude, the inner spaces where we are alone with ourselves, occurs every night when we are dreaming, whether we remember our dreams or not.

All life regularly sleeps, and during the solitude of sleep the activity of consciousness continues in the form of dreams. These are the times given to return to the perfect stillness. During sleep, while the body is resting, the silence draws closer and tends to every soul and spirit in nature. During sleep our being stirs while in solitude. Our whole mind awakens. The monk and mystic inside us is present. These moments of solitude give the mind the opportunity to experience itself, to integrate, balance, and remember its true identity.

Our dreams keep us attuned to the true mind, the mind that lives in the solitude of the unconscious dimensions.

Our dreams are much more than "just" dreaming. The silent worlds are participating with us whether we remember the experience or think we were "only" sleeping. Imagine the world without everyone at least sometime sleeping and without the silence restoring order between what is seen and unseen. In each dream's plot, in the unique landscape of our minds, the silence is balancing the energy between our soul and daily life. What is important is not necessarily the events occurring, the dream's story, but the energy that is experienced. The symbols in our dreams have different meanings for people in different life circumstances. But each symbol represents the unseen forces and elements of the silence in our subconscious and greater being. The symbols in our dreams each contain energy for us to accept and integrate into our everyday awareness. As we awaken to our dreams we become conscious of the part of our life that is in complete solitude, the part of us that is expressed in dreams. Each dream is another moment of personal silence. Every night we rest, our spirit opens and faces again toward the vast quiet. Much more is taking place than even most poets have the courage to imagine and write about. Many dimensions of love and fear, body and no body, our limitless and limited life, are interfacing.

At the beginning of rest the angel closest to us helps prepare our soul for the night. Special invitations are sent into the silence. Some people stay in their body and dream about an integraton of the day's events. Some leave their body for other realms in the stillness while their angel sits next to their side guarding them.

To discover what really happens when the body is sleeping is to discover the realms of the silence. This is why death is so often compared to sleeping. This comparison is more true than is often realized. In the great final dream, in death, the angel no longer waits

for our spirit to return to our body but flies away with
us.

―――――――

There are so many varied experiences happening in the event we call sleeping. The mind that is under control during the day is released to its entirety, to unending awareness. In sleep everyone surrenders to the silence no matter what they may think upon rising. The many realms of the intimate being are always caring no matter how limiting our beliefs or our religion. Deprive someone of sleep and they will eventually go mad. The silence is essential for our mental, emotional, and physical well-being. Souls on a spiritual path for a period of time may feel more and more like sleeping. Sleep can be a training ground where we attend "classes," remembering we can fly, breathe under water, walk through walls, and instantly communicate with whomever we wish. Whether or not we remember our dreams, their effect, their lessons, are influencing our day.

Before sleep, we can ask for a dream to help us understand a certain situation. We can ask for rest, peace, or whatever our life is most needing. The ability to dream consciously develops our evolving relationship with the silence. As we become closer to the stillness, and accept our dependence upon it, the silence can easily take us where we desire to be in our dreams, where control has let go to the quiet awareness within us.

―――――――

Dreams remind us that life is perhaps nothing more
or less than a dream, the awareness of the silence
dreaming through us . . .

―――――――

In dreams we meet the other personalities in ourselves and others. We can witness parts of ourselves that go unnoticed or that we avoid, like different desires, resentments, or anger. We experience other events in the night with the silence very close to us without our intellects and the forces of the day interfering. The other realms of our being are more accessible and can be more deeply experienced when our daytime awareness is not present to question. People who do not believe in life after death report profound experiences of visiting in their dreams with loved ones who have passed on and feeling better about the visit. People who are stuck in a certain life situation often report that they found the solution in a dream. Dreams are an avenue where the peaceful presence can be with us directly. Then it is up to our own will to feel and listen to what the dream says.

After learning about the silence, some people need less sleep because the intimate presence has interwoven their day and night, mind and spirit. Dreams are always happening. Life is a dream in which we encounter the silence in every circumstance, day or night. To become conscious is to wake up to the true dream. The silence in its many disguises is introducing us to our true wholeness for our acceptance. The monastery without walls permits us to dream and live our life as if it is truly ours, our dream to fully experience. Our everyday identity is integrated and changed in our dreams. The peace and love in the stillness can serve to help us collect the thousands of pieces of our fragmented being, until we are one soul again in the silence. One by one, each piece helps us discover our identity as a monk living in the monastery of expanded being without walls.

THE OTHER SIDE

In the quiet-filled life, we learn to include the other side, to open to and become aware of the invisible forces, to awaken to the dream in the silence. Life becomes sacred again as we become conscious of the many beaches of our mind in the ocean of the silence, as we become conscious of the love of the other side living amongst us.

The other side has been pondered by all religions of the world. People have returned from near-death experiences with startling stories. But the true beauty that waits for us is in many ways unfathomable, because we are not aware of the everyday beauty of the silence. We do not seek the extraordinary but discover the extraordinary living naturally within our lives.

The other side, the experience after death, the invisible presence with us, the other sides of our everyday consciousness including our dreams, are very close, becoming more familiar as we become familiar with the love in the silence. As we practice listening to the simple presence in the many rooms of our lives, we discover the many different sides to life. All are protected and held in the silence more than we imagine. Indeed each life is held and protected inside a prayer, which comes with us into the world from the silence. Beginning at birth our destiny, our inner being, are protected in the silence, held in this prayer. As we no longer hold onto our personality as our daily identity, as we feel ourselves in prayer and meditation, and open to the other side that is a part of us, we discover a prayer, a warm comfort around us, full of direction and wholeness. This prayer is a protective experience, holding our vulnerability, reminding us of our own divinity. Our soul lives surrounded in prayer. This prayer is the skin put around our souls, around heaven within us. As we depend less upon the world in front of us, our physical being, and personality we can feel our real support and this is the prayer God has placed around each of us.

All the different sides of awareness, the shorelines of consciousness, can lead us to this prayer about us. Perhaps this prayer is part of what some spiritual traditions describe as the akashic records or what others think of as part of the aura. Regardless of the name, we are born into the world naked but held in a prayer. And we live our lives with this prayer protecting and guiding us, and we return to the vast awareness still in this prayer and welcomed home. What we call the other side, the possible realms in the quiescence, is all in the prayer that is with each of us. This prayer is the skin of silence that surrounds all life and continues to be with us when we leave our bodies. As we become more conscious of the silence, we feel this prayer realizing that our physical skin is not our entire body. There is more. Our being is held in prayer.

The other side has so many properties, realms, and dimensions to experience that seem strange to us, but they are strange inasmuch as we remain foreigners to the silence.

THE AURA

Around every living thing the silence puts a special part of itself, an aura, to nurture and protect. The more time spent within the perfect stillness the more noticeable is this layer of special devotion that surrounds all life. The aura contains the record in the silence of each soul's past and options for the future. These "records" also known as the akashic records are kept close to inform and guide each person. The aura also contains an accurate reflection of everything that is taking place in our physical, mental, emotional, and spiritual life. Inside each aura are the means to reach out to other beings and energies in the vastness for support and simple companionship. The aura expands as each individual accepts more love in the stillness. The great saints could be felt from many miles away or by the mere mention of their names. This was because their participation in the pathways of the silence encompassed so much.

Whether we are saints or ordinary people, the silence is around us with a special presence, full of graces for each life in every time and setting. The lucid stillness feeds us through our aura and knows who we are, where we are, and what our needs and desires are. Our thoughts and feelings constantly affect our aura. Beings in other realms sense us and stay away or feel drawn to us because of the layer of silence that is uniquely about us. The subtle suggestions, the little intuitions, and the spiritual experiences that influence our day come from this part of the silence, the aura around us. The pure stillness is close to each of us through our aura. This special body of silence, our aura, is a wrapping full of details, including the veiled essence of where we come from and our purpose. Angels and souls of all kinds know us and serve us by the quality of silence our aura carries.

GUIDES

The monastery without walls reminds us to focus always anew on our interior being. Here we find the sacred silence that is rich in guidance.

All souls are given a guide to take them into the silence. Whether consciously felt or not, this invisible teacher is always with us representing the kingdom of the stillness. In addition, many people seeking direction are fortunate to have a physical teacher who guides them to feel and appreciate the silent mysteries. Such a teacher has to be sincerely requested so that the forces of the silence can make the necessary arrangements. There is a saying that when the student is ready the teacher will be there. Sometimes a teacher might be already with us, but we just haven't recognized him or her yet as our teacher.

It is important not to take such teachers for granted. It is important to show them our love and respect for what they give and share with us. In the course of our relationship with them we discover that our physical teachers are also human with weaknesses and prejudices and imperfections like our own. This does not make them any less of a teacher. The purpose of having a physical teacher is for us to learn to receive the best from him or her. We are not to confuse the teacher with what is being taught. Even Christ pointed the way to the Father. Like every relationship, the relationship between student and teacher reveals many mysteries of the wordless wonder. If the relationship concludes with any feelings other than respect and gratitude, then the relationship is not concluded. The silence does not give another teacher so quickly. If we look for a new guide while experiencing difficulty with our present one, we will forget that everything we seek elsewhere is already here. Our old guide is still inviting us to learn the lessons of forgiveness.

Our guides bring us the lessons about love and loving until we receive them in every part of ourselves and others.

Our guides in the silence are more than providers of gifts. They call us to live in the places where we find no gifts, including the ultimate place that is the source of all gifts.

The purpose of every guide is to support us as we find our true place in unfolding creation. We should judge our teachers by only one standard, and this is the path of love's prevailing truth and sweetness that is shown to us.

Eventually the goal of every student should be to share the knowledge, love, and wisdom he or she has received with others. Those who become a guide for others need to remember that they run the risk of becoming more important than the silence. This is why true guides teach by example. Many great teachers talk less and serve more. Others retreat even more into the quietude. As they talk and do less, their being is full of the tender laughter that reveals the great joy of the silent universe.

ANGELS

In the monastery without walls, we find blessings where we thought there were no blessings. We find angels where before we thought we were seeing only ordinary people or simply feeling a tender presence. The monastery without walls makes life safe enough for the angels to be close to us once again. Many people who have lived close to the silence have felt the presence of angels, but they have chosen to remain quiet about it.

The silence is crowded, full of angels. There are angels and there are angels. There are angels whose only purpose is to catch words that are true and take them someplace where they will be received. There are angels standing in front of the gate to every vulnerability. There are angels who stand tall to the sky and there are angels who live very close to the ground. There are angels for every need of the heart and desire of every child. There are angels who just watch the grass grow. And there are angels who watch over all kindness. There are angels for the weak and of course for all the homeless. There are angels who support our passage into life at birth and there are angels who hold us in their open arms at the moment of death. And there are angels who watch over our soul and comfort us during illness. There are angels for transitions of all kinds.

There is an angel over everyone. There are angels who light the path ahead. There are angels to help us sleep and angels to guide us once we are asleep. There are angels who inspire our plans. And there are angels who give the wisdom of not having plans but of living in the simplicity of the moment. There are many angels available in the silence around everyone.

There are angels for plants to grow. And there are angels for animals who become stuck in the mud. There are angels who live in the tops of trees and just on the surface of small and great bodies of water. There are angels who fly the distance between earth and the stars many times a day delivering messages. One angel may stay with one wildflower for its entire life. And another angel may assist the flowers in communicating with one another. Angels watch over all children and old people. And there are angels trying to teach others how to be more alive as if forever young. There are angels and there are angels, legions of them, large and small. A whole hundred angels may be present to protect one moment of love between two souls.

There are angels bowed in praise and angels busy passing on the great lights of the heavens. There are auras of angels around every saint, safeguarding their holiness, and passing on their love and joy to the world and the heavens. There are angels and there are angels. Some angels go places no other angel would venture. And there are angels who watch over angels on such missions. The realms of angels are always expanding in the silence. In all weather, in every season, there are angels. There are angels upon request and there are angels who need no invitation. There are angels and there are angels.

There are angels who give guidance and angels who help express gratitude. There are angels who protect and stand right next to the truth. There are angels who catch the tears that are shed and there are angels whose hands wait to touch an opening heart. There are angels who sit with children and old people to honor their solitude. And there are angels simply on the lookout to help celebrate joy. In the silence there are angels and there are angels. Wherever there is life there are angels nearby, in the quiet standing in reverence.

THE MONASTERY

The ancient monastery, often hidden in mountain valleys or in faraway deserts, was filled with experiences of sacred silence that remained virtually unknown to the world. Why would anything be said to a world filled with the noise of prejudice and lack of faith? Today our expanding awareness is not to change the world with intriguing stories of miracles and strange realms. We seek the love in the great stillness for no reason other than itself. This love in all its forms may be experienced in the heart of our spiritual practice, the heart of our lives committed to restore the sacred silence.

Whether through letting vows guide our life or fasting to purify it, our spiritual practice helps us see that the silent ways can be our ways. Whether we develop a new relationship with time to slip into the solitude of the moment or be more aware of our dreams to find new dimensions of oneness, our spiritual practice calls for increasing discipline of our entire being. The interaction of the love and the silent universe, and that of the prayer and the aura surrounding us, increase as we commit ourselves to a spiritual practice. Our guides and the angels who are with us are vital members of the monastery without walls. With no physical walls to contain our life, our spiritual practice is more important than ever in providing structure and foundation for our soul's journey through time. It is our spiritual practice that gives the concept of a monastery without walls flesh and bones. Our spiritual practice is what opens us to the pure sound in the silence, what changes our ideas about silence into direct experience. Our spiritual practice is what brings our awareness to the subtle worlds, the places that have the sweet presence our heart of hearts dreams of.

CHAPTER NINE

OUR SOUL AND THE STARS

Every spiritual practice that leads us further into the silence helps us experience our soul. The soul includes experiences of great peacefulness and visions of celestial realms as real as what we normally see. The soul is the joyful acceptance of everyday life and experiences of sustained ecstasy. The soul is an expanded quiet, feelings of great light and limitlessness. The soul is love's awareness of itself. Through prayer we can open to an entire cathedral of silence within us, our soul. Listening to a friend, walking in the woods, putting our child to bed, can be moments of wakefulness for our soul. Our soul makes ordinary reality sacred. Our soul's experience of the world is like the bond between a mother and her child. But the feelings of devotion and appreciation are not limited to family or friends but can be felt toward perfect strangers. All of life is important. Our soul feels and reflects the beauty of the souls we live with. Our soul's awareness does not begin or end with 'I' but speaks of 'we', encompassing every being around us. What we used to think of as self includes others, nature, the light of the stars, the pure sounds in the silence, love's touches through all our senses. The experience of the soul includes knowing how right everything is in our lives, including everything that is challenging us. Our soul gives us the sense of being guided into a life that is simple and naturally full of order. Our soul reminds us that love is always available. What is described as enlightenment is everyday experience being enlightened by the soul. Heightened experience of all kinds is the normal awareness for the life that has made a home for the soul.

The silence in our physical lives helps us remember that we are more than our bodies. We also have a soul, the part of us that is pure, lasting forever, which is the fresh breath of God. The awareness of silence in our everyday emotional and intellectual life helps remind us that we have more than a personality. We also have a soul. Our soul cannot be known, touched, or explored by any means other than love. All the different spiritual experiences we have serve to reawaken our knowledge of our true being, the life of our soul, the life of God within us. Our soul is purely God, the undivided self, the awareness of perfect beauty.

Some people lead very physical lives through athletics or healing from a bodily illness. They are learning the aspect of their soul that is their physical experience and how love can influence how they physically feel and act. Some people lead very emotional lives through relationships or, for example, with drug and alcohol problems. They are exploring the depths of their being and can learn how love can influence their emotions. Other people lead external lives very much involved with being successful or popular. Their being is exploring its relationship to others and to society. The harmony they find can lead them to the inner harmony and their soul. Every life experience can reveal different aspects of love, and through love we encounter more of our soul. The soul is as layers of love, one more pure than the other.

CONTEMPLATIVES IN THE WORLD

As contemplatives in the world, we are committed to knowing our soul through our awareness of the silence in every part of life. To uncover our soul we do not need the material walls of a monastery to safeguard our experience. It is our relationship with the love in the stillness that gives us new values, directions, and ways of being, which open us to our soul in the midst of a busy world. Instead of reacting to the noise around us, we seek the true sound, the pure sound in every voice we live with and hear through the day. Instead of always letting our fears lead us to needing more possessions or activity, the wholeness of our soul leads us to appreciating simply being instead. The path our soul takes is one of being a contemplative in the world. We pray for a life that is simple and true. As contemplatives, we are touched more by the preeminence of the silence than by the promises of the material world. As contemplatives living in all parts of society, we discover that the peace of oneness, the presence of our own soul, is calling us in all our activities, all of life's opportunities. Aspects of our wholeness are available in everything we do. All walks of life have the opportunity to experience their soul, particularly as they revere their lives and those around them.

When viewed as aspects of our soul to experience, life's joys and challenges can be gifts toward greater wholeness. Each experience can give us new terrain of love for our soul to discover. As wholeness that is separate from the silence is neither real nor wanted, wholeness that is separate from discovering our soul is not possible. Our freedom comes from accepting our interconnectedness with the sacredness in the silence in all of life. As contemplatives, we live absorbed in the silence where we separate our fears from love's awareness.

———

As contemplatives, we are commonly finding a new moment in our day full of the fresh presence of beautiful grace. We collect our joys and our shadow and bring them to these unifying silent moments. Our soul is felt in our interrelationship with all and every-thing. Love's simplicity gives us the strength not to turn away from our experience but to go toward heart-filled moments wherever they may be.

As contemplatives, we are humbled to include the sense of the sacred in the experience of our everyday senses. Within the sacred we find ourselves feeling, caring, and being more. Our soul is present. As we are empty, open, and available for the unspoken essence, we can encounter our soul in almost everything we do, in whomever we are with.

As traditional monks and nuns are required to find the balance between intense activity and simply being, between creating and listening for the source and guidance for creation, we are required to find the same balance. Some-times our physical needs move us and sometimes we find our physical needs are not as strong as the fears that are busy in them. Sometimes the depths and heights we find in prayer hold us in perfect communion. And at other times these same depths and heights are moving us to become active and giving in the world. As contemplatives, we find that there is a season for going into the cave of our interior silence to experience the purity of our soul. And there is another season for going out into the silent wonders to discover our soul's breath of love in the world. In either season, our fears are fleeing to the eminence of harmony and the awareness of our soul expanding.

THE GREAT SAINTS

As contemplatives, we learn that the great saints are our teachers. They are the people who committed their lives to discover their true nature, their soul. The saints grew to realize they could not live separately from their soul as if it did not exist. They knew that humility, simplicity, and devotion helped them feel their own divine being. They knew they had to give their life away as much as they could in order to possess the true life, the life of their soul. The great saints in all their rich experiences give examples of how to find our way into the silence, how to find our way to the seat of our soul.

Many of the great saints chose to live with the poor, the lonely, and the sick because they knew the most naked had nothing between them and the silence. Other saints preserved their intellectual life for only contemplating silence or preserved their sexual desire for only desiring the love in the silence. There were saints who consciously gave their physical lives and died for their beliefs in the presence of love's perfect oneness. They knew that love would protect and care for their soul. There were saints who cared for hundreds, created religious orders, and built vast institutions, as if all their activity was possible only if they were in attunement with their soul's light and destiny. There are saints who did very little for others. They simply humbled themselves to receive the most pure love pouring out of the silence into their soul. These were the saints who recognized the quality of being a saint in others. They loved the courageous ones who, through their loneliness, poverty, illness, and simple life, reflected to the world how lonely, poor, and ill we are in a world without love, and how beautiful life can be with the love in the silence.

For this reason Saint Francis and other great saints wanted to live with the poor, the lepers, and those who were on the very edge of life, barely surviving. This is where they found their soul. They recognized that by giving into the temptation to be comfortable, they were often settling for temporary comforts instead of the ever-present comfort that comes from feeling the nakedness of the soul in the care of the vast love in the stillness. Saint Francis kissed the leper on the lips as if knowing he was kissing a part of himself, as if knowing how misshapened he was without love in his life.

With love every circumstance in life is simply another opportunity to discover more of the soul and where our soul and God are inseparable.

The saints taught us to seek out first the love in the unsounded and then focus on our daily comforts. This way our needs diminish as the silence assumes more space in our life. The saints seemed to discard all concerns about everyday existence, but only after they found how much their everyday life is supported and cared for. They discovered how loved they were in the stillness. The great saints discovered how every soul is loved. Then they threw themselves upon the heart of the silence for their daily needs. Secretly they smiled, knowing this was not a risk at all, for in truth there was nothing else to depend upon but the sacred wonder.

HOLINESS

The great saints learned that the true clothing of the soul was holiness. The experience of silence is clothed in holiness. It is holiness that protects us, nurtures us, and calls us to seek out the simple presence in every part of life. We live in a culture that is very critical of the word holiness. Our suspicions and doubts about the holiness of others are often obstacles to experiencing the holiness of our own being.

As Mother Teresa of Calcutta frequently says in her public talks, "Holiness is not a luxury. It is not the privilege of a few. Holiness is our simple duty." She then proceeds to talk about holiness evolving out of action, our acts of love. Most people are not interested in holiness because they think they could never feel so much love or become so loving or holy. So they give up. But holiness is not the result of a certain quantity of love. Holiness comes through the quality of love we are willing to feel and to give. Mother Teresa says, "Holiness is our simple duty because we all have an obligation to love, because we are made in the image of the Divine."

Holiness itself is not ours to have or have not. It is a state of being. It comes from the silence. Holiness is the gift of protection that surrounds every soul who opens to the vulnerability of love. When love becomes our desire, the motive behind our actions, the purpose of our day, holiness is present. Each intention of love is a step toward holiness. Each act of love is holy. As we love we are putting our commitment to know and live in the sacred into action. As our soul calls for the silence to become omnipresent in our life, holiness reigns.

Holiness is the aura the silence puts around the pure in heart. Holiness represents the truth of love's presence, the perfect joy offered in every life circumstance. To be holy is to give the silence free reign in our lives. Many contemplatives have experiences of holiness that are the gifts they receive for giving up their need for self-importance, unnecessary abundance, and recognition.

Holiness is the gentle feeling that touches us when we are in a difficult situation. Holiness is when our children say thank-you and sincerely mean it. Holiness is the sense of purpose and destiny, the soulful feeling we have when we are in the perfect place at the perfect time. Holiness is seen in wise old women's eyes in the marketplaces in faraway countries and felt around the simple fishermen in their small boats as they pull in their nets.

Holiness is present at every dawn and at every sunset. Holiness is in every sincere act of love. People who give easily are frequently put off by words about holiness but feel at home in the experience. Holiness is too full of silence for words. Holiness is in nature that is left undisturbed. Holiness is what touches someone in need when we give to them without thinking of ourselves. Holiness is what touches us when we receive from others without any expectation. Holiness is the clothes given to the soul brave enough to show himself or herself completely.

Flowers serve no greater purpose than to reflect the many colors and scent of holiness. Children are naturally innocent until the noise of the world confuses and distorts them. We can see the innocence of their holiness leave their faces as if they are being pulled from inside themselves. Holiness is still in them but has been overshadowed. They may have to wait for the cycle of life to bring them to old age when we all are a little more wise, simple, and available for holiness.

Holiness is close to every soul who feels life on course, filled with purpose. Holiness is in the rain, the snow, every season for the person who embraces his or her own seasons. For such a soul holiness is in the riches and poverty of life, during times of illness and physical wholeness.

Holiness is always within us. People willing to claim it discover that it grows as they give of themselves. Holiness is the memory of that pure place every soul carries inside. Sooner or later all souls remember there is no replacement for holiness. Holiness is in the very essence of the silence, and life simply is incomplete without it.

Holiness is in the smile we wear and the tears we shed. Holiness is in the smile we appreciate on others and their tears that we care for.

———

Holiness is the unifying experience that introduces us to our own soul. Wholeness that is separate from holiness is like a personality without a soul. Holiness is the guiding force, giving us the grace-filled moments that help us to receive our true self. Our souls are illuminated in holiness as we rediscover our part of the creator, our part of creation.

Holiness is the framework for the soul's awareness, whole and emptied for life's sacred oneness.

WHAT'S INSIDE THE SILENCE

The saints demonstrate the life of holiness that is possible in all of us. We discover the lives of the saints as we discover what is inside the silence, as we open to the richness and vastness of our own soul, love's interior life. As we learn to treasure our inner awareness, we become aware of the treasure, the immense love, the intense light the saints found. They could not turn down any other path if it took them from their first and only love, the sacred silence.

As we become sensitive to our soul's experience, we find the smallest moments, the slightest breezes, can move so much inside us in the stillness. Life's brief encounters with intimacy have more importance. With the subtle qualities we find in our inner life, the silence leads us. The pure presence always begins inside. From our soul's quiet recesses we are taken to caverns and gardens and skies above mansions of silence.

Our interior life is full of the ways of the soul. Our dreams, feelings, intuition, and thoughts are just the beginnings of the vast language of our soul in the silence. In our meditations and prayers we hear the small whispers the perfect presence speaks to us, seeking our awareness and appreciation. To value our inner life is to open the doors for the galaxies of stars in the silence to be discovered. These stars turn out to be not so far away but right next to our soul and in the midst of the hearts of those around us.

Each of us in our interior life has the perfect map to discover our soul. Our conscious experience, moment by moment, leads us where we want to be. The temptation is to value just the easy, comfortable parts of our inner being and ignore the rest. The temptation is to be busy seeking new experiences instead of feeling all the depths and the corners of our life experience now. Our interior life is the fresh breath of our soul. We cannot be too aware, too conscious of the movement of our being and the silence within us, the silence in all things.

BEAUTY

Our interior life brightens with every discovery of beauty in our lives. A very clear and joyful way to knowing our soul is to become aware of the beauty within and around us. Every moment of beauty appreciated in the world is a reflection in the divine mirror of our soul. The beauty we see in others and in nature is a part of our own being. Our soul and beauty are inseparable. A life committed to viewing simple beauty regularly has shown us a path rich in the sacred awareness.

Beauty is full of silence. Wherever beauty is beheld there is love surrounded in stillness. Religious icons have long been appreciated as pathways into the silence, keepers of sacredness. The beauty of nature, a walk with a friend, and a child in his or her spontaneous wisdom are full of the presence of silence. The beauty in great and simple art brings us closer to more of life's inherent beauty. Simply being aware of the beauty around us is a true way of living in the monastery without walls. Beauty touches more than our ideas and feelings. In some inexplicable way it touches the prayer that is around us and our soul. Each of us depends on having beauty in our life whether we are conscious of it or not. Wherever we encounter beauty it expresses the sacredness of the unseen harmony. Life's beauty, like the silence, goes often unnoticed. But when appreciated and sought for, beauty can be a way of viewing images of love in the vast stillness; it can become a pathway for awareness of many reflections of the divine in our soul.

Recognizing the beauty of the souls we live with can lead us to the beauty of silence. Seeing the beauty in nature's seasons, in how we dress for one another, in the manner we prepare and serve our meals, and in simply having fresh flowers in a room helps us to keep in touch with life's sacred monastery and leads us to be conscious of the magnitude of our soul.

Making the details of our lives beautiful can be a sure way of affirming the presence of beauty always around us. Making our days beautiful is a way of building a life worthy of our soul, making it right for the beauty of our soul to be present.

OUR SOUL AND THE STARS

We are inspired with more beauty as we change our perception of ourselves, partners, and community. The limited image we have of ourselves affects our view of everyone else and the world around us. Our physical strengths and weaknesses, our feelings and moods, our everyday thoughts and fantasies, and our abilities and faults are just a small part of our entire being. With the silence included in our life, we come to understand that we have a soul that interrelates with everything seen and unseen. We are part of the great mystery of love. Sometimes we are hungry for love and at other times we are fulfilling the need for love in others. Sometimes we are feeding the people before us with our love and other times we are nourishing the unseen yet present beings in the silent dimensions. As much as our soul has a destiny beyond physical life and death, our being has a history, a past that includes much more than our early childhood. The history of our soul is found in the silence within us, the prayer around us, and the simple presence we each have in the world. The details of our past, the specifics of our soul's journey, may not be so important. But we can remember to give each other more respect because our body, our personality, our life, are the result of evolution since creation itself.

As we perceive life's offerings and treasures differently, we perceive the people we live with in the monastery without walls differently. As we value these people less for what they can or cannot do for us and more for what they are and bring to us, we can begin to appreciate the interior universe lived in and explored by everyone. The people we live with are expressing their current integration of love's presence in their thoughts, feelings, hopes and fears, their search for their soul's essence in this moment in the silence.

As the presence of love's oneness is increasing in our life, we become sensitive to the unique presence each person offers. The silence found in ourselves opens the door of silence in those around us. During lunch with a friend, an hour of play with our child, a meeting or sport activity, we can become conscious of the people we are with through our hearts instead of through our intellect or emotions judging them. As we learn to be present, their special beauty, their silent being, become evident. In our emptiness we become available to how each person touches us. We can become aware of the souls we live with. We can learn to enjoy their special presence of silence. As we take the time to enjoy and become sensitive to one another, we discover that each soul has a presence, a way of being that can be felt in terms of a quality of light. Each soul has a quality of light, a light that can be as soft as a candle or as piercing as a spotlight, subtle, strong, open, or dense and heavy. All souls in our life have their own quality of light that touches us, warms us, and affects us much more than we are usually conscious of. It is time to awaken to the presence of silence and the quality of light in the people we live with. It is time to receive and appreciate their special energy in our life, their unique wave of light, and to realize how each person influences us. It is time to awaken to the stars not only in the heavens but also in our midst. In each one of us, within our bodies and personalities, and around our soul, there is a light, perhaps an original wave of light from the star from which we come.

All people in our life are much more than the label we attach to them: friend or relative, cook or salesperson, secretary or teacher. They are much more than their likes and dislikes, their present trials and pleasures. They are more than an ego or a personality. The silence introduces us to the soul in each person in our life, and with the guidance of the silence we feel the essence of a star, the subtle wave of light with every soul. The light of silence introduces us to the silent light in each other. As we give less thought and attention to how agreeable or difficult the other may be, the silence in each soul stretches over the personality, past daily life to our true dimensions. The light of the silence stretches and connects to the stars, to the particular star that each soul comes from. To know someone in the intimacy of shared silence is to meet a star, the unique light that has developed with his or her soul full of the learning process.

As theories in physics tell of the universe being blown apart in a "big bang," perhaps the original light that unified us all was separated just as suddenly, in the same moment. Perhaps the unifying experience we seek, the intimacy of simply being together we desire, is from this original separation. Perhaps consciousness experienced a big bang and was broken and spread across the universe. Maybe our souls were spread out of this consciousness and light, each a small piece of the divine. Our soul is our part of the pure heart of God. We were spread through the cosmos by a divine breath. Then slowly a personal history, our spirit's individual traits, grew around our soul.

Meanwhile our life, the people around us, those who are drawn to us or feel pushed away, are a microcosm of the universe. As we expand in consciousness, our desires contract to wanting what is genuine, essential, and necessary. The people in our lives are parts of the stars gravitating to and from each other. As we receive each other's light and consciousness, the love, we can collect the light of the stars as we appreciate the souls in our life. Perhaps each of us is here to collect stars, to help weave the fabric of the universe back together again. We are here, challenged to affirm the original love that holds all the realms of life and being as one.

_____

Love's perfection pays no attention to the surface of our lives but is known underneath, in the energy, the basic path followed in each life. Every soul literally comes from the stars, and our purpose is to represent our star in the great unification of the earth and the heavens.

In the silence we can feel each star serving its earthly purpose and carrying the dream of returning home. Beginning with each cell in our body, we carry the cellular message of our cosmic origins. As scientists are finding that the genetic code carries so much information of who we were and are, it is possible for us to find our place in the cosmic silence. On earth, the stars are meeting, and it is only a matter of time before the silence will give us the answers about where we really come from and are going to. The answers come as we open to the magnificent present. The answers come as the presence of silence assumes its rightful reign in our lives.

_____

Life in the silence can prepare us to meet the stars we live with every day but have not seen. The silence takes us beyond our human judgments to the unique body of light each life expresses. The silence awakens us to our true purpose, and this is to be our true self, the light of the star surrounding our soul reuniting in heaven.

The day is coming when we will no longer resist anyone in our life but will be more receptive to what he or she is bringing to us. Each soul coming from a different star brings a different quality of light and love that creates a specific awareness, all an aspect of the most pure, God. Some bring love that is strong, others a love that is compassionate. Some bring love that is wise, soothing like a warm sea. Some can bring love that shakes us like a difficult truth to hear, or love that is childlike, gentle, like a sweet fragrance. Some may bring a tender, caring hand from a star full of such caring. No matter what appears in the personality, it is only a temporary small cover over the star from which we come, from the star where our soul resided after being born out of God's breath. And now our personality is the unresolved aspect of our star's journey that has emerged in this lifetime. One way to heal our egos or personalities is to become aware of just how much they are only a small part of our entire being. With the help of the silence, our personalities cease to dominate, and our star, the light about our essence, is shining out from our souls more than ever.

The silence is blanketing the earth and making it safer for more souls to remember where they come from and why they are here. Every time we risk to feel the love of others, the light of their star joins us. As we resist less what life brings to us, we feel more of the unique love coming from each person. Slowly the light of the stars is meeting inside our hearts, making each of us whole and connected with the universe.

If we think about it, each person in our life touches us. We can feel each person in our bodies in a unique place. No two people touch us in exactly the same place. Nor do we feel any two people in the same way. It is no accident that we turn to one friend for compassion, another for understanding; to one for play, another to challenge us. It is the meeting of the stars that is really taking place. Different qualities of light are merging, healing, creating wholeness, and unifying the fragments of our consciousness. These qualities of light have been refined and synthesized through our relationships, our spiritual practice, through the life of our soul. We are called to prepare for each human encounter as a meeting with the divine. As we open to the divine in each other, life's noise has fallen and silence has assumed its place.

The people we are closest to, our parents and family, have the greatest influence on us. We are sensitive to their most subtle expressions and behavior. Each family, a cluster of stars, is a family projecting fear and love upon its members. As we love our fears, the fears of the others have less influence on us. As we become more conscious of the presence of silence, we can safely open to their particular starlight no matter how fearful or close to their starlight they may be. Perhaps it is because of their starlight that we were born into our family. In our families, the challenges or difficulties we experience are ours to heal in the great healing of consciousness. Anything short of seeing the divine, the light of the stars, in our parents and family is short of seeing the truth. As long as we are concerned with ourselves, defending ourselves, making the other person wrong, we have not let the silent presence assume its place, touch and heal our lives. We have not opened to the final stages of healing the noise of the past with forgiveness, love, and service. The monastery without walls calls us to the unique silence, the presence of the star, the divine in those closest to us.

As we make room for the silentness in our lives, we are stopping the old patterns of living separate from our soul. We are establishing new ways of being for ourselves and those around us. As we forgive and appreciate our parents, we offer them the opportunity to forgive and appreciate their parents. Healing has no boundaries in the silence. We can only imagine where healing truly begins and ends. Opening to the love in the people closest to us can change their thoughts and perceptions of the people closest to them, even if not consciously at first. Since addictions, habits, and abuses can be passed from generation to generation, healing our relationships not only stops the destructive process in the present generation, but also sends the presence of healing through our parents to their parents and on to their parents and so on. In the silence, in the realms of consciousness, our ancestors are not separate from us. The bonds between us and the souls departed, with all souls, are great and live on in the silence. In continuing healing how can we say it is too late for forgiveness and love, when we believe in the soul and the survival of physical death? In the silence our ancestors are present and perhaps waiting to be released from the fearful bonds and the bonds of guilt that hold them so they too can expand into more light. Our ancestors are not far from the doorway into the silence that our spiritual practice takes us to every day. Their presence, their love are part of the great love that the silence offers to heal our hurt, our noise, in perfect quiet. As the souls of many generations are touched by one true soul, our soul in the silence can play an unlimited role in the great healing. It is never too late to restore the simple presence of love. Our prayer, our awareness in the silence, touch all beings. Our ancestors may be waiting for our conscious efforts, our forgiveness. Our ancestors may be waiting for us to receive their love, the love they had hidden behind their fear-filled personalities at the time. In the silence beings are lined up, praying their love will be received. And each moment we are available, all love received helps another to be in greater consciousness and greater light. Our ancestors are intimately involved with us in the silence. And as we embrace the path before us, there is no saying how many beings may be on the same path literally with us, appreciating that we are present for them, with them.

As one member of a family changes, all members are touched. As one soul hears itself and becomes free from the bonds of noise around it, who can say how many other souls, how many generations, are released in the same moments of liberation? As the love between us survives physical death, the love between generations past and present is an unending bond, a spiritual cord that keeps us forever connected. The humility and respect, the devotion and care, we open to can reach to

many souls in the silence. Similarly, many souls in the
silence who have discovered their light wait to share
with us their newly found illumination. Our dreams,
meditations, prayers, and daily life can be open for our
ancestors and generations to come. The past is healed
in our healing. The future is set free in our liberation.
Our loved ones past and future are a part of us, with
us, intimately involved in the silence of our soul.

As we live closer to the silence, we have more of our
authentic being and less influence from our everyday personality and that of those around us. Fear becomes translu-
cent when we don't give it the weight of our perception.
When we live in the silence, we can reflect our star and peer
into and receive the light of the stars of those around us.

With our spiritual practice, the prayer of silence around
us, we can be open and vulnerable for love. The simple and
pure light of others can be directly received and appreciated.
The closer we live to the silence, the closer we can be to the
silence in all who are with us. Their fear, their personality,
are no obstacles as our fear, our personality are little more
than a small cover to the depths of our soul and the starlight
within. By receiving who we really are, our fears and daily
dramas become less important. The souls in our life now are
more relevant. Our awareness of their light, what their
presence has to give us, is important for our own wholeness
and for finding the heavens within us. All souls in our lives
can play a special role in enlarging us to more being and
love. The silence helps us become sensitive to the true light
around us, the love of a beautiful star in everyone in our life.
The monastery without walls is the home we make for the
stars. Our interior life can be empty for the great reunification of the stars to take place in. Each of us can remember
and help restore the sacred to consciousness, to every part
of our life on earth and in the cosmos.

OUR STAR IN THE SILENCE

Many of the world's religions name the great star that calls to us, the star of peace. Religious leaders through time speak of the perfect star in the silence and pray for its arrival or return. Underneath different rituals and customs, people everywhere are seeking the one starlight, whose essence is full of promise. What is important is not necessarily the words that we attach to the most pure love but our spiritual practice to receive it and our daily life of giving to others. We all are a part of the great universal drama in the silence. Many, many souls are consciously participating, joining in the prayer for all beings, the prayer for the one star, the one light that will bring all souls to love that is already unifying peace within so many corners of the world. As we risk to become the presence of the starlight within us, we open to the one great star that brings all light together.

In the midst of the noise and confusion of everyday life, each of us is the light of a star that shines within us, that pulls us closer to our place on our pathway in the unsounded wonder, to the place where we come from and where our soul was created in God's breath.

Our star is found in the silence among all the stars as we find our spiritual practice, our words, and our being, which is true. Each day, each path we follow into the silence peels away more of our separateness. The walls we have built around us become less necessary as we feel the monastery without walls protecting us. The love of the silence takes our human walls down slowly, showing the prayer around us, the star within us that is moving us to the one light that gives order to all consciousness and the cosmos.

We are called to be our unique presence, the love the simple quiet reveals within us. On our intimate pathway, we feel the gravity, the pull of our star and those of others. Our intuitive wisdom speaks to us. On our path in the silence there is a bright star shining over our head. This is the star that protects us, guides and supports us to fulfill our essence in life.

———

The soul that finds her star in the silence bows in humility knowing her life is on course, full of everything that is important for her to be wholly herself. Everything needed, including the shelter, food, companionship, strength and courage is given to represent the love of the stillness, beautifully, gracefully, with all her being.

———

THE MONASTERY

The time has come for consciousness to gain its preeminence over the struggle for daily needs, for the pure sound found in the silence to transform the noise we live with. We know that by developing our capacity to give and respond to life in every form, to all beings and species, our earth in its critical condition can be healed. Through this process we can realize an incredible peace. As the monastery of all religions has traditionally been the keeper of the sacredness of the silence, now is the time for all of us to risk finding this sacredness, which can restore nature and bring the dignity that will restore the human being, our soul, and the star within us.

———

We are called to be collectors of silence, to recognize the moments between moments, the presence that says everything without words, that gives and gives with no need of recognition. As a world of nuns and monks living the life of ordinary people, we are collecting the silence, witnessing the silence, giving refuge to the silent love, risking to make our life one of grace. We are living our lives committed to restoring the peace of the earth, committed to restoring her delicate balance of life, the air, fire, water, and minerals. The attention we give to the silence honors the earth and the prayer that surrounds her and all of us. Meanwhile, in holy appreciation the earth gives herself to be the place for the reunification of the stars of heaven. The earth gives herself as the place where the pure essence of our souls can be rediscovered through each experience of faith and love. In the monastery without walls we receive each other as souls, the stars of heaven, celebrating life in the silent joy as we reunite with the infinite.

ABOUT THE AUTHOR

Originally trained as a psychologist, Bruce's spiritual development has led him to value the presence of the soul. Through the years working with people from many backgrounds and countries, he has developed a unique gift of helping others find their most genuine path and spiritual experience.

As husband, father, teacher, therapist, retreat leader Bruce is committed to restoring the sense of the sacred in everyday life. He is very thankful for the many people who have given to him and joined him with their commitment, risking to listen and live in the monastery without walls.

Bruce Davis, Ph.D. is also the author of *The Magical Child Within You, The Heart of Healing* and *My Little Flowers* which he considers his most inspired work, a book of daily meditations.

Bruce leads spiritual retreats in many different parts of the United States as well as Europe. Each year people from several countries join him on pilgrimages to Assisi, Italy the home of Saint Francis and Saint Clare as well as other sacred places. With his family, Bruce lives in Marin County, in the San Francisco Bay Area where he teaches and has a private counseling and healing practice.

For more information about Bruce's retreats, counseling, and current activities please write: Spring Grove, P.O. Box 807, Fairfax, California 94930.